REMEMBERING PHIL ESPOSITO

P. ESPOSITO

REMEMBERING PHIL ESPOSITO

A CELEBRATION

CRAIG MacINNIS, EDITOR

RAINCOAST BOOKS

Vancouver

Raincoast Books gratefully acknowledges the ongoing support of the Canada Council for the Arts; the British Columbia Arts Council; and the Government of Canada through the Department of Canadian Heritage Book Publishing Industry Development Program (BPIDP).

Raincoast Books
9050 Shaughnessy Street
Vancouver, British Columbia
Canada V6P 6E5
www.raincoast.com

In the United States:
Publishers Group West
1700 Fourth Street
Berkeley, California
USA 94710

Library of Congress Number: 2003091879

National Library of Canada Cataloguing in Publication Data

Remembering Phil Esposito : a celebration / Craig MacInnis, [editor].

ISBN 1-55192-639-3

1. Esposito, Phil, 1942- 2. Hockey players--Canada--Biography. I. MacInnis, Craig.

GV848.5.E68R45 2003   796.962'092   C2003-910375-7

Printed and bound in Canada.

1 2 3 4 5 6 7 8 9 10

ART DIRECTION AND DESIGN: BILL DOUGLAS AT THE BANG

For photo credits, see p. 114

CONTENTS

*Sharp-dressed man:
Espo ties one on.*

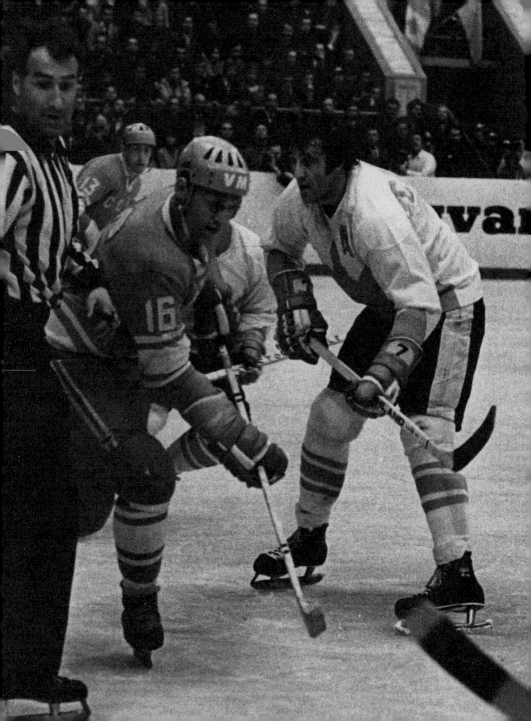

TOASTING THE TEAM OF THE CENTURY
BY CRAIG MacINNIS

WHEN THEY GATHERED TO REMEMBER their greatest month as players, it was, fittingly, Phil Esposito who spoke last.

"Every time I'm with these guys there's a special feeling," Esposito told his audience. "We had a tremendous run. There were a lot of things that happened, a lot of things that ... are we proud of? Maybe not, but we did what we had to do to win, and for that I am very proud."

"He was their leader then, and he speaks for them now," Canadian Press veteran hockey journalist Neil Stevens wrote of Esposito's words that night in September 2002 at the 1972 Team Canada 30th anniversary banquet.

Most of the players from the original roster of 35 were on hand, and so were 300 people who paid to dine with them in a hotel in the featureless suburban sprawl near Toronto's Pearson International Airport.

As a media event it might have lacked the glitz and immediacy of Canada's gold-medal victory at the 2002 Winter Olympics, but it's probably safe to say that Paul Henderson's 1972 series-winning goal against the Soviets, and Espo's famous quip — "When he scored, that's the closest I ever came to loving another guy" — comes nearer to defining Canada's hockey spirit than anything accomplished by Wayne Gretzky's admirable charges in Salt Lake City.

Showdown: Esposito eyes the puck as Vladimir Petrov (16) leads a Soviet breakout in the '72 Summit Series.

One was a major sporting event with strong nationalist overtones, the other a defining moment in the country's hockey life — a down-to-the-wire test of Canada's mettle on the international stage and a Cold War duel that just doesn't seem possible to repeat in this era of Russians on virtually every NHL roster.

Thirty years after winning their showdown with the Soviets, it seemed only right that Canada's players got rings bearing the inscription TEAM OF THE CENTURY.

"It comes at a good time, because my knuckles have got a little arthritic so my Stanley Cup ring won't fit on that hand," said Esposito. "I needed another ring, and I got it. It looks good, and it feels good."

As Neil Stevens noted in his piece for Canadian Press, "it was Esposito who took the reins. He played the best hockey of his career and led the team in points with 13."

Espo, of course, went on to manage the New York Rangers and the Tampa Bay Lightning. He has long been a resident of Florida, where he works as a TV commentator at Lightning home games. But none of that matters, really. His name will always be synonymous with the single greatest sporting achievement by Canadians in the 20th century.

"Somebody once said nothing lasts forever, but I'm starting to think this does," said Harry Sinden, referring to the legendary team that he coached.

He is probably right.

The Dynamic Duo: Espo and teammate Bobby Orr take a breather between the action.

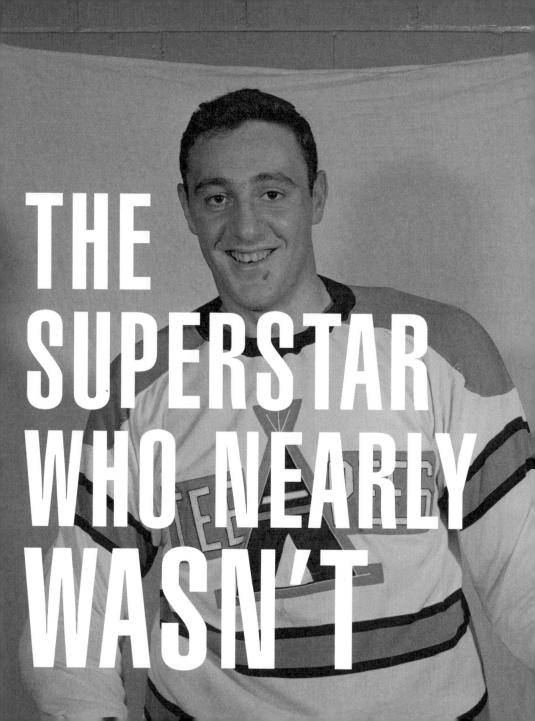

THE
SUPERSTAR
WHO NEARLY
WASN'T

HOCKEY'S GREATEST LATE BLOOMER

BY CRAIG MacINNIS

HOCKEY'S FUTURE GIANTS are almost always spotted on the horizon, tearing up the peewee leagues in their hometowns, rewriting the record books as junior stars in places like Oshawa, Swift Current and Penticton.

Like gymnastics and classical piano, hockey tends to nurture prodigies — young stars such as Gretzky, Lemieux and Lindros, Dionne, Lafleur and Orr — whose careers seem a fait accompli long before they don the sweaters of their respective NHL clubs.

Given the game's long-standing love affair with precociousness, the most notable thing about Phil Esposito's career might very well have been its slow, unsteady ascent. Seldom has greatness taken so long to find itself.

According to *Time* magazine, Espo spent most of his childhood winters in Sault Ste. Marie on double-runner skates — he got up at 6 a.m. with brother Tony to practise before school, but "failed to make the local bantam team on first try." At 14, "he fought his way into the midget league, only to be cut because the coach was convinced he couldn't skate." By 18, Phil had also failed to make the Junior A St. Catharines Teepees, a farm club of the Chicago Black Hawks and the final proving ground for youngsters hoping to make the pros.

He settled instead for $15 a week as a Junior B player in Sarnia, where,

New recruit: Phil, 19, models his new
St. Catharines Teepees jersey in the fall of '61.

according to *Toronto Star* sportswriter Milt Dunnell, "he was no better than a 50-to-1 shot as a future big-leaguer."

Undaunted but overweight, the big kid from the Soo was back at the Teepees' tryout camp the next September, determined to make the team as a 19-year-old rookie. According to Phil in his 1971 book *The Brothers Esposito*, the Teepees' legendary coach, Rudy Pilous, delivered an ultimatum that would light a fire under the pudgy recruit.

"Hey, Fatso," barked Pilous. "You want to make this team of mine?"

"Sure," said the young Espo, skating over to the coach. "What do I do?"

"Lose some weight," Pilous said. "Get down to 200 pounds by the start of the exhibition season and you've got a job."

Showing early signs of his remarkable will, Esposito promptly went on a starvation diet. "It was tough," he recalled. "I'd watch the other guys eating hot dogs and drinking milkshakes and go nuts. I didn't eat between meals and at dinner I'd just have a piece of steak."

By the morning of the Teepees' first exhibition game he had managed to starve himself down to 201 pounds, which was good enough for Pilous. He offered Espo a contract that nearly quadrupled his Sarnia salary — a grand total of $57.50 a week.

In a game against a Senior A team, the new Teepee scored five goals. "Right there in St. Catharines the road opened up," Phil said. "I was on my way to the big leagues."

Those familiar with Espo's career path know there would be other hurdles along the road to superstardom, but those early, formative years as an unwanted prospect gave him a keen edge that helped him battle through the rough times.

Sweater exchange: Espo, modeling the team's new Hawk uniform, with Teepees teammate Bill Ives.

UNDAUNTED BUT OVERWEIGHT, THE BIG KID FROM THE SOO WAS BACK AT THE TEEPEES' TRYOUT CAMP THE NEXT SEPTEMBER, DETERMINED TO MAKE THE TEAM AS A 19-YEAR-OLD ROOKIE.

To wit: In Game 2 of the Boston Bruins' opening-round series against the New York Rangers in the spring of 1973, Espo's season ended abruptly when he tore ligaments in his right knee. Without him, the Cup-defending Bruins crumpled like an empty duffle bag, falling to the Rangers in five games.

"I knew it was serious the minute I went down," Espo said later. "I could tell right away." He underwent surgery at Massachusetts General Hospital, just around the corner from Boston Garden.

"The doctors had told me there was no reason why I couldn't play again — as good as ever," he told a reporter. "But there's always that nagging fear in your mind. I finally told myself, 'Look, it didn't seem to figure that you were gonna be a big leaguer in the first place. If you're through now, everything that's happened is a bonus.' That made me feel better."

WHEN WE THINK OF ESPO'S LINGERING HOLD ON THE COLLECTIVE PSYCHE OF HOCKEY FANS — HIS TWO STANLEY CUPS; HIS RECORD-SETTING 76 GOALS IN THE 1970–71 NHL SEASON; HIS HEROIC ROLE IN TEAM CANADA'S VICTORY OVER THE SOVIETS IN THE 1972 SUMMIT SERIES — MUCH OF IT SEEMS EXPLAINED BY HIS "ORDINARINESS."

Lacking the pure athletic genius of his great Boston collaborator, Bobby Orr, or the end-to-end dazzle of his former Chicago linemate, Bobby Hull, Espo got by on qualities that seem more in line with the values of the average North American — a proud work ethic, a sense of humour and an unabashed desire to succeed. Maybe that's why we couldn't help but love him.

In *Time*'s cover story on Espo in October 1972, writer Bob Lewis itemized the player's achievements in the then-recent series against the Soviets: "No one invested more of himself than Phil Esposito, the series' top scorer, who emerged as the natural and acknowledged leader of the team."

"Espo's was a Protean performance: his bulky six foot one-inch frame seemed to be everywhere at once, shoveling passes to the wing, bearing down balefully on the referees, fighting remorselessly in the slot, even metamorphosed as his brother Tony to appear behind goalie Ken Dryden and block an otherwise certain goal in the climactic last game."

He was us. Or at least an idealized version of what we would like to be — an average guy who became a legend by the sheer force of his will, with an outsized personality and the constitution of a dray horse. Oh, and one other thing: that Midas touch in the slot.

Prettiness never factored into Espo's craft. When he was in Chicago, he was labelled a "garbage player" because of his knack for scoring in ugly goal-mouth scrambles. "I don't care if the puck goes in off my head," he told *Sports Illustrated* at the height of his fame.

His rough-and-tumble play, it could be argued, changed the way the game was played from Montreal to Moscow.

In a critique of the Soviet-Canada series for *Sovietsky Sport*, a Soviet coach, Nikolai Ephstein, wrote: "The defencemen of the Canadian team are highly efficient and play accurately at the close approaches to the cages. It is true that in their goal crease they tend to violate the rules and operate roughly. In conditions of such tough and close-marking defence, the individual skill of the forwards acquires great significance, and from this point of view, the Soviet players have something to learn from Phil Esposito."

We loved him because he was never guarded in his enthusiasms, never held his tongue when a good diatribe was in order, never shied away from playing the clown when fate flung a banana peel at his skate blades.

One of the most memorable images of Espo during the Canada-Soviet series is from a pregame tumble he took as he skated onto the ice in Moscow for Game 5. The image is unforgettable to those who witnessed it: the self-deprecating Canadian, willing to make a joke at his own expense, injecting levity into a tense situation.

"I tripped over the stem of a flower the little girls skated out and gave us," Espo recalled. "Part of the stem of mine came off and fell on the ice. Now I'm introduced and skating back to the blue line and I find myself falling. What can I do? Everybody's laughing, and I'm laughing myself, flat on my back. I get up and give them a big bow."

It was before the next game, however, that he cinched his rep as hockey's master comic. Pretending to be worried that he might repeat the gaffe and take another spill, he carefully clung to the boards during his introduction. It was much the same in Boston, where his humour and tenacity were the glue that bonded the Bruins during their run for the Cup in the 1969–70 season.

"The Bruins have been likened to the old Yankees because of their depth of talent, and to the old [St. Louis] Cardinal Gashouse Gang for the laughing way they go to work," baseball author John Devaney wrote in1970. "Esposito keeps them laughing, and around him the others cluster, something they have been doing since he joined them three years ago and made them believe that the last-place Bruins could be Stanley Cup champions."

Along The Boards: Phil wheels past Leafs defenceman Borje Salming in a game against Toronto.

ALTHOUGH IT WAS PAUL HENDERSON'S GOAL THAT SEALED THE VICTORY FOR CANADA IN THE FINAL MINUTE OF THE FINAL GAME, IT WAS ESPO WHO EMERGED AS THE TEAM'S SPIRITUAL LEADER, ITS HEART AND SOUL. ITS GUTS.

Fall 2002 marked the 30th anniversary of Team Canada's win over the Soviets, and it is safe to say that Esposito's performance in that series remains a benchmark against which all other Canadian hockey performances are judged.

During the 2002 Winter Olympics in Salt Lake City, when the Canadian men's hockey team lost their opening game to Sweden (before turning things around and claiming the gold medal in their win over the U.S.), Canadian defenceman Al MacInnis made a postgame plea for calm. His words were simple but direct: "This isn't the first time a Canadian team is going to take heat and it won't be the last. We'll deal with it. There's a lot of hockey left to be played."

In the media, MacInnis's mild speech earned instant comparisons to Espo's plea to a nation after Game 4 of the Canada-Soviet series in Vancouver, which stands as the most impassioned soliloquy in the history of the sport.

In excoriating us for losing faith in a team that had stumbled during the crucial rubber match on Canadian ice (a 5-3 loss, leaving the series 2-1-1 in Russia's favour as the clubs headed for Moscow), Espo brought us together in a way no politician, priest or poet could. Shaming the boo-birds and inspiring his psyche-battered teammates, he set the table for Canada's amazing comeback during the Soviet leg of the tournament, in which Canada won the final three games by one-goal decisions.

Although it was Paul Henderson's goal that sealed the victory for Canada in the final minute of the final game, it was Espo who emerged as the team's spiritual leader, its heart and soul. Its guts.

Following the series, a cartoon by the *Toronto Star*'s Duncan

Where were you in '72?: Esposito, Paul Henderson (19) and the rest of Team Canada mob goalie Ken Dryden after Game 8 in Moscow.

Macpherson captured the national mood. It showed a smiling Espo sniffing a rose, over the caption: "Canada's First Italian Prime Minister."

The kid who'd been cut from midget and junior teams — who'd been written off as too slow or too heavy — had somehow found the will to persevere. "He was passed by because he was an ugly duckling," said Hockey Canada director Doug Fisher. "He could have been a hockey dropout."

In pictures and words, *Remembering Phil Esposito*, the fifth title in our continuing series on NHL legends, offers a nostalgic look back at the career of one of hockey's 20th-century giants, a pure goal scorer and a pure-hearted leader of men.

Hockey Hall of Fame writer Frank Orr weighs in with a definitive entry on Espo's 1972 performance in Moscow, describing in sequence the greatest week of Espo's career. In another chapter, Orr pays homage to the so-called Sultan of Slot, analyzing the tactics of the Bruins' vaunted offence with Espo terrorizing goalies from the doorstep of the crease.

Orr also looks at the deal that took Esposito to Boston from Chicago in 1967, considered one of the most lopsided in the history of the sport, as well as the trade that sent him to the New York Rangers eight years later.

ESPN's Rob Adler gives us an unvarnished look at the trigger-happy exploits of Espo as a general manager in New York and Tampa, where he earned the nickname "Trader Phil" for his habit of dealing players as if he were a 10-year-old collecting hockey cards. Espo, it is safe to say, was as active a GM as he was a scorer.

Doug Herod offers a different angle on the Espo legend. Herod admits having no use for the Big Bad Bruins of the early 1970s, but he was forced to

THE KID WHO'D BEEN CUT FROM MIDGET AND JUNIOR TEAMS — WHO'D BEEN WRITTEN OFF AS TOO SLOW OR TOO HEAVY — HAD SOMEHOW FOUND THE WILL TO PERSEVERE.

change his mind when Boston's rangy superstar led Canada to victory over the Soviets. That's a familiar sentiment for many hockey fans from Canada, who hated Espo as a Bruin (mainly because he was fattening his scoring totals at the expense of the Leafs and Habs), but came to admire his patriotic leadership in the '72 series.

We also take a peek into the season-closing weeks of the 1970–71 season, when Espo set a new NHL standard with his 76 goals, a record that would stand until it was shattered by Wayne Gretzky, who notched an incredible 92 goals in the 1981–82 campaign.

As the editor of *Remembering Phil Esposito*, I hope what emerges from this colourful collection of articles and vintage pictures is a fresh sense of what made Phil Esposito one of the most compelling athletes of his generation — not to mention one of the bravest and most beloved.

Thank you, Phil.

Ranger Phil: Former Bruin Espo in unfamiliar red, white and blue.

ESPO MOVES TO BEANTOWN

A MONSTER IN BOSTON

BY FRANK ORR

AS THE STORY GOES, a rival general manager paid a backhanded compliment to Tommy Ivan at the NHL's annual meeting in June 1967.

"Everyone in the league says thanks, Tommy," the man said to Ivan, GM of the Chicago Black Hawks. "You created a monster in Boston."

The previous month, Ivan had made the trade that sent forwards Phil Esposito, Ken Hodge and Fred Stanfield from the Black Hawks to the Boston Bruins in exchange for centre Pit Martin, defenceman Gilles Marotte and goalie Jack Norris. The three large forwards were important parts in the creation of the Big Bad Bruins, who went from awful (missing the the Stanley Cup playoffs for eight consecutive seasons from 1960 to '67) to awesome (rewriting much of the NHL scoring record book en route to Stanley Cup triumphs in 1970 and '72).

To most hockey observers, it was shocking news that the Hawks would move three big, talented players developed in their farm system at a stage in their development (Esposito was 25, Hodge and Stanfield 24) when they seemed ready to graduate from high potential prospects to front-line regulars on a contending team.

The Hawks claimed they filled a need by adding Marotte, at 22 a well-regarded defence prospect. He would bolster an aging back line that would

Top: Espo takes his seat in Boston
Bottom: As a Hawk, battling Habs' Jacques
Laperriere and J.C. Tremblay for the puck.

be made thin in that year's first NHL expansion draft. The Hawks also got goaltending depth in Norris and a sound two-way centre in Martin, but the fact is that personalities, more than on-ice ability, inspired the trade.

The Hawks were truly "old school" under the ownership of the Wirtz family, who entrusted their hockey operations to two career-NHLers, GM Ivan and coach Bill Reay. The latter was a serious, somewhat dour man who wanted his players to be devoted, hard-working and silent. Reay and Ivan had an especially thorny relationship with the fun-loving, fast-mouthed Esposito.

"The front office and Reay had little regard for the three guys they traded to the Bruins," said a man close to the team in that era. "They figured Espo was a big goof who wasn't serious enough and didn't produce when the heat was on, that despite his size [six foot one, 205 pounds] Hodge physically was a 'soft' player who sulked when things were not going well, and that Stanfield's offensive potential was limited, at least not as high as his big numbers in junior hockey indicated it might be."

Even Bruins GM Milt Schmidt admitted doubts about the deal when he made it, despite peers calling it "highway robbery" against the Hawks.

"I was reluctant to include Marotte in the deal because he was a good prospect out of our system. In Gilles and Bobby Orr, we felt we had the backbone guys for a top defence for years when they matured," Schmidt said. "Martin had been a solid forward for us and Norris had showed potential in junior and minor pro ranks. But we had small forwards and getting three good-sized guys was important. Esposito already had showed the tools of a good NHL centre."

In much of the two previous seasons, Esposito was centre on a line with

Long reach: Esposito keeps the puck away
from Leafs defender Allan Stanley.

BUT FROM THE TIME HE CRACKED THE HAWKS ROSTER IN THE 1963—64 SEASON, ESPOSITO FELT THAT HIS TIME WITH THE TEAM WOULD NOT BE LONG.

"FROM THE START IN CHICAGO, I WAS CALLED A 'GARBAGE COLLECTOR' FOR BOBBY HULL," ESPOSITO SAID YEARS LATER. "SURE, I SCORED SOME GOALS ON THE REBOUNDS OF HIS SHOTS BUT, MOSTLY, I WORKED LIKE HELL FOR MY GOALS.

the league's top gunner, left-winger Bobby Hull, and industrious right-winger and fellow Sault Ste. Marie product, Chico Maki. Hull had scored 54 and 52 goals in those two seasons and later called Esposito "my right arm." The Hawks were the NHL's highest-scoring team, led by Hull and his young linemates plus the "Scooter Line" of Stan Mikita between Ken Wharram and Doug Mohns.

But from the time he cracked the Hawks roster in the 1963–64 season, Esposito felt that his time with the team would not be long.

"From the start in Chicago, I was called a 'garbage collector' for Bobby Hull," Esposito said years later. "Sure, I scored some goals on the rebounds of his shots but, mostly, I worked like hell for my goals. The first guy to tell you that I helped Bobby Hull was the man himself.

"But I butted heads with Tommy Ivan and Billy Reay right from the start. Hey, it wasn't all one-sided, either, because I was a bit of a wise guy and didn't always live by their behaviour rules. I wasn't a great skater, a bit slow off the mark, not all that agile, and I occasionally lugged a little extra weight."

Esposito figured his problems with GM Ivan started with his first professional contract after his one season of major junior (then Junior A) hockey with the St. Catharines Teepees team that produced many Black Hawks. Ivan offered a signing bonus of $500 and a salary of $3,200 for the season. Esposito held out for $1,000 to sign and a $3,800 salary.

"I stuck to my guns and, in the end, they gave me what I asked for," he said. "But they made me feel that I had robbed the office safe. I think Tommy Ivan labelled me as 'trouble' at that point."

After a productive season and a half in the minor pro ranks, Esposito was summoned to the Black Hawks during the 1963–64 season. Esposito acknowledges that coach Reay leaned on him about his skating speed and inspired a devotion to improvement. But he was used only in spots, behind centres Stan Mikita, Bill Hay and Chico Maki, and the $7,500 minimum NHL salary the Hawks paid Esposito was well below the salary and scoring bonuses he could earn in the minors.

Early in Esposito's first full NHL season, 1964–65, Reay moved Maki to the wing and made Esposito the third-line centre. When the team had a slow start, Esposito was placed between Hull and Maki. The "HEM Line" was born, scoring strongly from the start as the Hawks went on a 13-game unbeaten streak.

After the Hawks eliminated the Detroit Red Wings in a seven-game series to open the 1965 playoffs, several players had a celebration in a Detroit hotel room.

"We drank more than a few beers and had a loud bitching session about Billy Reay's shortcomings as a coach," Esposito said. "We didn't know Reay had changed rooms and was next door. First chance he had, he told me that he had heard every word said about him."

Although the Black Hawks lost a seven-game Stanley Cup final to the Montreal Canadiens, the future appeared bright for Esposito, who had 23 goals and 55 points in his first full season, 10th among NHL scorers.

"The next season (1965–66) got away to a lousy start for me," Esposito said. "I broke my hand in a dumb exhibition game fight with Bryan Watson [of Detroit] and played in a cast. Of course, I had problems even after the cast came off, and Reay moved me off the big line. Then Maki and I, who were roommates, overslept and were late for a practice in Toronto. Luckily for me, Maki was a Reay favourite so we got away with a $100 fine each but the coach was all over me after that."

A favourite of Reay — and every other coach and GM, for that matter — was Mikita, the gritty little centre who had already won two scoring titles, would win two more plus the Hart Trophy twice as most valuable player. He was a first all-star six times. Born in Czechoslovakia, Mikita was brought to Canada as a child and was in many fights with needling kids.

"Stan and I are friends now, but when I was a young player we didn't get along very well," Esposito said. "Reay used him as an example in the shots he took at me. He made it sound like I grew up as a pampered rich kid, who got everything easy, while Mikita fought his way to the top. Through his first six or so seasons in the NHL, Mikita was regarded as the dirtiest player in the league. When Reay told me I should have that sort of attitude, I said it was possible to be a nice guy and still play good hockey. He told me I wouldn't be around the game long if that's how I felt. I told him we'd see about that."

Esposito bounced back from the hand injury and had a decent season, scoring 27 goals while partnered with Hull, who scored 54 times in breaking Rocket Richard's record of 50. Hull actually had tied the record by slightly deflecting an Esposito shot into the net, but he refused to take credit for the score.

In the 1966–67 season, the Black Hawks finished first for the first time in the franchise's history. Esposito had a 21-40-61 point total and Hull scored 52 goals; the Hawks placed four players on the first all-star team, defenceman Pierre Pilote and forwards Hull, Mikita and Ken Wharram.

"I drank too much champagne at the party to celebrate the pennant. It

*Wraparound Attempt: Esposito eludes
Leafs rearguard Tim Horton while
Eddie Shack guards the post.*

made me brave and I did a dumb thing," Esposito confessed. "I always was timid around Tommy Ivan, but not that night with a snootful of booze. I said to Ivan, 'We have a dynasty here. Don't screw it up!'"

In the first playoff round the Hawks were eliminated in six games by the elderly Toronto Maple Leafs, led by the goaltending of two ancients, Terry Sawchuk and Johnny Bower.

"I tried my hardest but I had no points in that series," Esposito said. "Add shooting off my mouth to Ivan and I figured I was finished in Chicago. I knew for sure when I went to Ivan's office to get my expense money for the trip home and he wouldn't see me. He told his secretary to get me out of there. I knew I would spend the summer waiting for the call about a trade and, really, it was my own fault.

"Well, I didn't have to wait long. On May 15, my wife called me at a friend's house and told me I had been traded to Boston."

"BOBBY HULL GAVE ME THE BEST ADVICE WHEN I CALLED TO TELL HIM ABOUT THE TRADE. HE TOLD ME, 'GO TO THE BRUINS, PLAY YOUR ASS OFF AND SHOW [THE HAWKS] WHAT A MISTAKE THEY MADE.'"

Straight statistics supply the best evaluation of the trade. Esposito, Hodge and Stanfield collectively played 1,725 games for the Bruins, scored 883 goals and 1,312 assists for 2,095 points. In the playoffs, the numbers were 212 games, 97 goals, 132 assists, 229 points. Esposito was NHL scoring champ five times, most valuable player twice and earned eight all-star team selections, six of them to the first team. Hodge earned two first all-star team spots. The Bruins won the Stanley Cup in 1970 and '72.

Martin was a good centre for the Hawks. In 740 games he had 234 goals and 304 assists and in 80 playoff games he had a 26-25-51 point total. Marotte spent less than three seasons in Chicago, racking up 10 goals and 63

assists, and was traded to the Los Angeles Kings in February 1970 in a six-player deal. Norris played 10 games in the Hawks goal in injury call-ups, registering a 3.95 goals-against average over seven games in 1967–68, and a 6.0 average in three games the following season.

But that didn't end Esposito's involvement in blockbuster deals. Early in the 1975–76 season, the Bruins and New York Rangers, two top

Welcome to Boston: Former Hawks Ken Hodge (left image) and Fred Stanfield (taking face-off, right), joined Espo in Beantown.

Hoist 'em high: Esposito and New York teammate Ron Greschner (opposite page) celebrate a goal against the Winnipeg Jets.

ESPOSITO AND VADNAIS WERE STRONG FOR THE RANGERS, LEADING A TEAM THAT LOST IN THE CUP FINAL TO THE CANADIENS IN 1979.

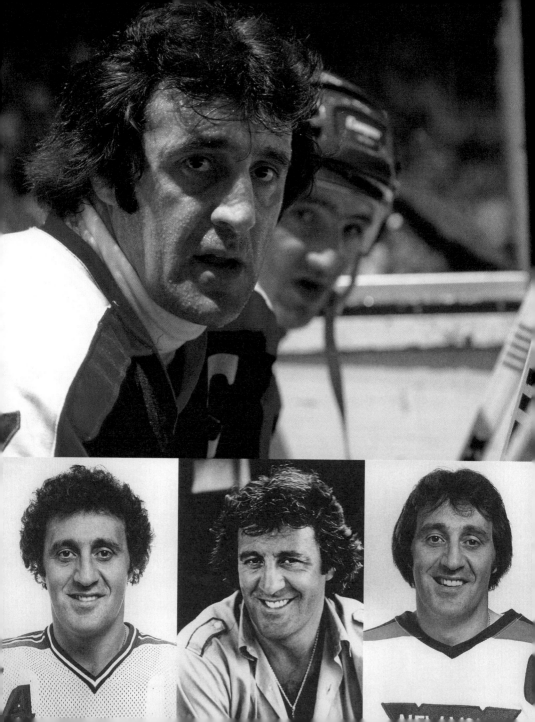

contenders for several seasons, were brushed aside by the pugnacious Philadelphia Flyers and the powerhouse Canadiens team taking shape in Montreal.

That inspired GMs Harry Sinden of the Bruins and Emile Francis of the Rangers to swing a heavyweight swap. The Bruins sent Esposito, who had scored 61 goals the previous season, and defenceman Carol Vadnais to the Rangers for centre Jean Ratelle, defenceman Brad Park and throw-in defenceman Joe Zanussi, who claimed he was the "biggest spare tire in NHL history."

The deal helped both teams. Esposito and Vadnais were strong for the Rangers, leading a team that lost in the Cup final to the Canadiens in 1979. Ratelle and Park led another strong run for the Bruins and were impressive replacements for two great stars, Orr and Esposito.

Espo took a while to get used to New York but eventually came to love it. "I've never had as much fun in my life, not even when I was with the Boston Bruins and we were winning the Stanley Cup," he said before the 1979 final against the Habs.

"This Ranger team has the same good thing we had with the Bruins in the early 1970s — an all-for-one approach. Cheap-shot one of us and you cheap-shot all of us. The only thing that matters is what the team does. I know that sounds corny and old hat but that's how it is."

Frank Orr covered the 1979 Stanley Cup final between Espo's Rangers and the Canadiens. Montreal won in five games.

Hockey head: The many hair styles of Phil.

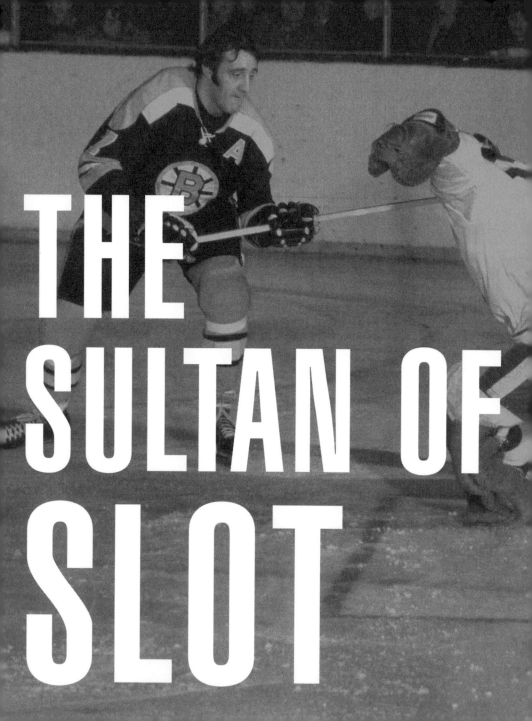

THE
SULTAN OF
SLOT

TRENCH WARFARE

BY **FRANK ORR**

THAT ELUSIVE QUALITY known as "scoring touch" comes in various guises.

Rocket Richard drove for the goal off the wing, fired shots on the fly or held off defenders to reach the net and jam the puck in.

Bobby Hull and Boom-Boom Geoffrion moved down the ice and unloaded high-velocity slapshots with big backswings.

Little Camille Henry flitted around the goal crease and through it, collecting "garbage" by tipping in a mate's shot or tapping in a rebound.

Steve Shutt and Jari Kurri both had the uncanny knack of finding open ice in the attacking zone and an ultraquick shot release, the unloading of a "one-timer" without requiring true possession of the pass.

Marcel Dionne and Gilbert Perreault would wheel and stickhandle through defensive coverage and go one-on-one with the goalie, beating him with a wrister or a soft-handed deke.

Mike Bossy, Wayne Gretzky and Guy Lafleur were among the versatile few who owned the complete skills to take what became available and turn it into a score with an accurate wrist shot, a well-placed slapper, a backhand shot while curling out of the corner, a flip shot from in close over a prone goalie, or a slick move in close to score on a short shot.

The men who had set the standard for NHL goal scorers over the years each had a distinctive style of placing the puck in the net, an asset or a move that they employed to score the majority of their goals. But until he made the area in front of the opposition's net — a minefield for attackers, known as "the slot" — his personal property, no big gunner produced goals in volume the way Phil Esposito did. In fact, no shooter previously had produced the Esposito scoring numbers by any means. Before he came along with his 76 goals in the 1970-71 season, the highest season total was Bobby Hull's 58, set in 1968–69.

THE "SLOT" IS NOT A DEFINED AREA LIKE A FACEOFF CIRCLE AND DISAGREEMENT EXISTS ON ITS MEASUREMENTS.

But, loosely defined, if lines were painted angling toward the boards from the goalposts, even from the outer edge of the goal crease, ending when they touched the "hash marks" of the corner faceoff circles, with a cross-ice line joining the dots, that would be the slot. Often a scorer will be in the faceoff circle when he connects, but the true slot is in that smaller area, directly in front of the goalie where the four corners of the net and the space between the goalie's pads — in hockey jargon "the five-hole" — are available as targets.

"Directly in front of the net, from 10 to 15 feet out, was the best place to be, the spot that gave you the most alternatives for scoring a goal," Esposito said. "But at the same time it was the toughest place to stay, the one where you took the most abuse. Often, the coverage forced me off to the

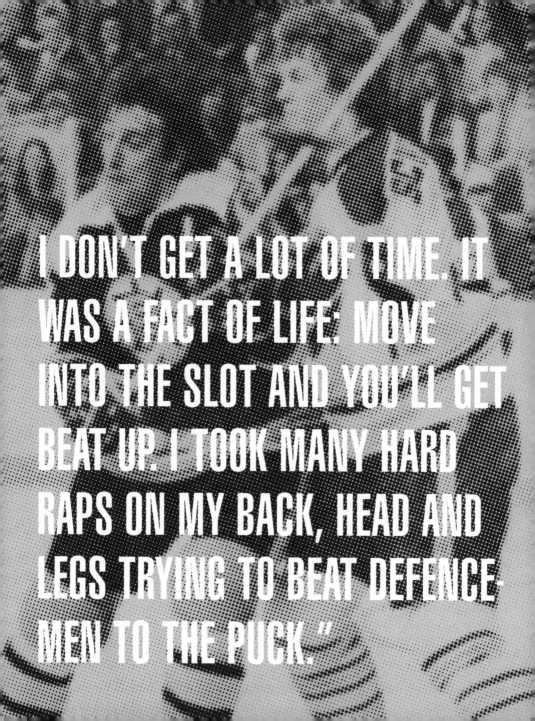

"I DON'T GET A LOT OF TIME. IT WAS A FACT OF LIFE: MOVE INTO THE SLOT AND YOU'LL GET BEAT UP. I TOOK MANY HARD RAPS ON MY BACK, HEAD AND LEGS TRYING TO BEAT DEFENCE-MEN TO THE PUCK."

side, where the scoring angle wasn't as good. The goalie would have the short side of the net covered and to beat him to the long side required a very hard, accurate shot. When I was squarely in front of the net, I had more targets to aim at.

"The slot could be called 'Death Valley.' Quickness is everything in there. If the defenceman is quicker than me, he'll clear it before I can shoot. I don't get a lot of time. It was a fact of life: Move into the slot and you'll get beat up. I took many hard raps on my back, head and legs trying to beat defencemen to the puck."

Through much of his time with the Boston Bruins, Esposito played at centre on a line with wingers Wayne Cashman and Ken Hodge, two large — and in Cashman's case, belligerent — wingers. They were masters of the corners. Hodge often carried the puck deep, holding it until Esposito was "at the desk in his office," then placed it on his stick for a quick shot. Cashman was the prototype for the classic "corner man," a strong, abrasive forechecker, all elbows and stick, gaining control of the puck with persistent digging. Often, when Cash made the pass to Esposito in the slot he would head for the front of the net to engage a defender in a diversion-creating, screen-building tussle.

Then, of course, there was "Four," Bobby Orr, the Bruins' sublimely gifted rearguard, the greatest offensive defenceman the game has known. Orr's incredible creativity, much of it based on his near-spooky physical skills and his instinct for divining what form each play would take, played a large role in Esposito's goal bonanza. But by the same token Orr claimed that his winning two NHL scoring titles — among the most extraordinary feats in team sports history, likened to a pitcher leading major league baseball in

*Mano a mano: Esposito battles
Buffalo's Jim Schoenfeld.*

homeruns — was the result of Esposito's offensive choreography and the defensive attention the centre was given.

"If I had the puck at the point, there was a complete list of possibilities for what I could do with it," Orr said. "Ken Hodge would be in one corner, ready for a pass which he would take to the net himself, give back to me or place on Phil's stick. Cashman would be in close to the net, raising hell, the perfect screen and distraction if I decided to shoot. And Phil was in the slot, and I knew if I put the puck in the right place I very likely would get an assist.

"Phil took incredible punishment to hold his patch of ice. He really paid a price for many of his goals. After games, I would look at his body all black and blue, like he had been beaten with a baseball bat. But he would simply absorb the crap to get the puck and shoot it.

"Phil's quick release of the puck once he got it was no accident. He worked hours and hours to develop his 'snap' shot. In reality it's a wrist shot, executed with a snap of the wrists and stick movement of only a few inches, because to have any windup at such close quarters wasn't possible if he wanted to get the shot away.

"Very seldom did he not stay on the ice after practice and work on his shot for 15 or 20 minutes. He never just dropped a pail of pucks on the ice and shot them. He tried to duplicate actual game conditions for his drills. He would have somebody — a teammate, a trainer, a rink worker, whoever was available — passing the puck to him, and he would try to control it with his skates as often as he did with the stick. Because his stick was tied up, hooked or held so much, he had to control the puck with his blades. When he had more than one volunteer, he would have the passer in the corner and a checker crowding him in the slot, forcing him to work at getting the puck and delivering the shot."

While many Esposito goals were the result of his staking a claim in the slot, his "original rush" output was high, too. Of course, moving up the ice in a wave that included a sizable segment of the NHL all-star team was not exactly a disadvantage.

A familiar picture from those Bruin glory days has Orr acquiring the puck behind his team's net and moving slowly with it through the defensive zone while his mates accelerate up-ice in their own lanes, Esposito striding in the middle, Hodge seemingly loafing on the right flank, Cashman, not a smooth skater, threshing along on the left. Orr's defence partner, Dallas Smith, also was usually ready to be a trailer on the play, a useful safety valve if he were the most open of the attackers.

Over-concentration on Orr in the defensive alignment meant that he could pass off — to Esposito gliding toward the line, or to Hodge, who would swing wide toward the boards to spread out the defence. Alternatively, a cross-ice pass to Smith would mean four top scorers were circulating without the puck or, if other avenues were closed off, a shoot-in around the boards to the far corner, where Cashman would arrive with his aggression — not to mention his elbows — at a high level. Orr occasionally would cross the blue line and stop with the puck, giving the forwards the opportunity to prowl and find open ice, qualifying for a deadly Orr pass.

But if the opposition's defensive alignment devoted too much attention to covering the other Bruins, that made room for every team's worst nightmare: cruising room in the attacking zone for Orr and his diverse attacking repertoire. He could flit into the open space for a deadly shot at the net, he could do a give-go-get, a quick pass to Esposito or Hodge, a jump into the

Slot Machine: Espo pots another one from his favorite location.

WHILE MANY ESPOSITO GOALS WERE THE RESULT OF HIS STAKING A
CLAIM IN THE SLOT, HIS "ORIGINAL RUSH" OUTPUT WAS HIGH, TOO.
OF COURSE, MOVING UP THE ICE IN A WAVE THAT INCLUDED A SIZABLE
SEGMENT OF THE NHL ALL-STAR TEAM WAS
NOT EXACTLY A DISADVANTAGE.

clear and a return pass for a shot. Or he could simply start a move toward the net, which would invariably cause the opposition to throw bodies in his path. Having lured the defence to his lane, Orr could calmly slide a pass in the slot to Esposito, who would snap a shot on goal.

"I've never argued with anyone who said that I was fortunate to have played as many seasons as I did with Robert Gordon [Orr]," Esposito once said. "What he did was create an edginess in the opposition when he moved with the puck, because when he was cruising into their end with it, every possibility that ever was — or would be — was on the table.

"But I take great pride in the fact that I wasn't exactly a dead weight on his back or Bobby Hull's when I was with the Black Hawks. Those guys always gave me a lot of credit for their success and that's a good feeling — to have two of the best few that ever skated pay you a tribute."

Phil's brother Tony — a goalie and NHL star in his own right — was, of course, a major booster of his brother.

"By making an area of the ice, the slot, into his own preserve, the first guy to do it, Phil really was a hockey pioneer," Tony said. "Others have tried to duplicate what he did, the way he scored goals, but not very many have mastered it to any level remotely approaching what my brother did. Phil had it all — the size, the guts, the determination and, most important, that unbelievable hand quickness to make it work."

Veteran sportswriter Frank Orr was inducted into the Hockey Hall of Fame in 1989. A longtime reporter for the Toronto Star, *Orr covered Esposito as a Black Hawk, a Bruin and a Ranger.*

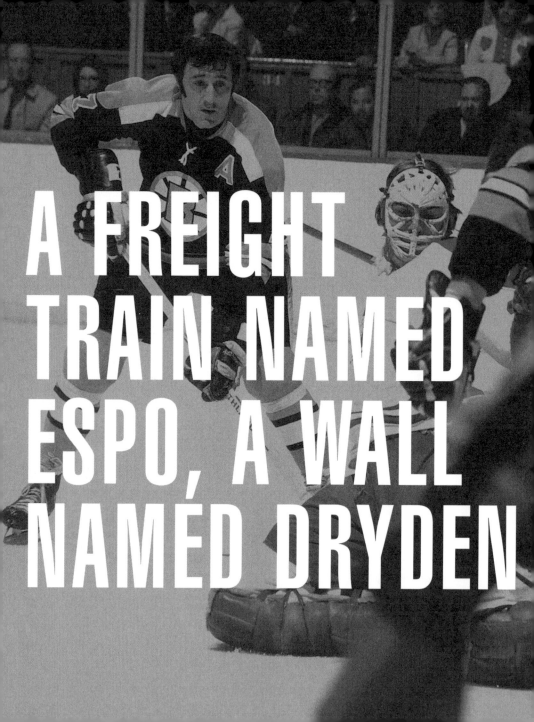

A FREIGHT
TRAIN NAMED
ESPO, A WALL
NAMED DRYDEN

ESPO SETS THE GOAL STANDARD

BY CRAIG MacINNIS

"I SUPPOSE I'M PREJUDICED, but I think our line has to be perhaps the greatest in hockey," Ken Hodge said on the night of March 31, 1971, as he and his Bruin linemates, Phil Esposito and Wayne Cashman, rolled like a freight train toward their presumed date with destiny — a second straight Stanley Cup for Boston.

It was not to be. A rookie netminder by the name of Ken Dryden would derail the Boston locomotive a few weeks later when Montreal surprised the heavily favoured Bruins in a seven-game quarter-final, but it was a heady spring nonetheless for Espo and his teammates.

On the night of Hodge's boast, Boston had just dumped the Habs in a late-season contest, 6-3. Hodge had collected three assists to set a season record for points by a right-winger with 104 (on his way to a 105-point finish), while Cashman picked up a goal and two assists, lifting his season points total to 77 (on his way to a 79-point close).

And Espo — well, what could be said about Espo? He had already shattered Bobby Hull's single-season goal-scoring record in a game on March 11 against the Los Angeles Kings when he fired his 59th goal — a nine-foot tip-in of a Ted Green point shot past goalie Denis DeJordy.

Espo got his 60th the same night, with plenty of time left for more.

"I'm glad it's over," he said after notching numbers 59 and 60. "With 11 games left after this one, I knew that sooner or later I'd get it."

The rest of the world could only watch and marvel at the apparent ease with which the Bruins accumulated personal scoring honours that spring, led by Esposito.

By the closing weekend of the 1971 NHL season, Espo had collected 71 goals — 13 more than the record Hull had established three years earlier — with games still to go in Toronto against the Leafs and in Boston against the Habs.

Before the Toronto game, Espo put his feet up in his hotel room and held court for the press.

"Nah, I don't feel any pressure at all," he told writer Jim Kernaghan. "I'll admit getting the 59th was a little tough. Once I got to 50, I never realized things would go this well, so there's really no pressure now.

"I don't think goals all the time, but I shoot a lot — Bobby Hull always said the more you shoot, the more you'll score. I've had more than 500 shots on goal this season."

And he still had a few more shots left on his stick. Espo went out and scored five more goals in the two weekend games, including three in a 7-2 romp over Montreal on the last day of the season. His total of 152 points on 76 goals and 76 assists shattered his own mark of 126, established two years earlier.

The NHL Top 10 in scoring that year was a veritable Bruinsfest. Defenceman Bobby Orr was right behind Esposito in second place with 37 goals and 102 assists for 139 points, a career high for Orr. Also making the Top 10 — Johnny Bucyk (third place with 116 points), Ken Hodge (fourth

Split decision: Habs goalie Ken Dryden blocks the lane as Esposito waits for a pass.

place with 105), Wayne Cashman (seventh with 79), and Johnny "Pie" McKenzie (eighth with 77). The only non-Bruin in the Top 5 was Espo's old Chicago linemate, Bobby Hull, who finished with 44 goals and 52 assists for 96 points.

Little wonder Espo felt so confident headed into that year's playoffs and the Bruins' defence of Lord Stanley's mug. "If we play like we did during the regular season, nobody can beat us," he predicted. "There's no doubt about it. We just can't let up."

Esposito felt that the return of Orr, who had been allowed to rest during some of the team's final regular-season games, would be the ingredient that put the Bruins over the top in the postseason.

"They always put a checking line against Kenny, Cash and myself, but no team can control everybody and when Bobby comes on the ice they can't do anything, the way he controls the game," Espo said. But that was before they met the Habs, who outscored the Bruins 28 to 26 in the seven-game series, including a 4-2 win right in Boston in Game 7.

"OKAY, THEIR ENTIRE TEAM PLAYED WELL," SAID A DEJECTED ESPOSITO. "BUT DRYDEN DECIDED THE SERIES. HE NEVER CRACKED, NEVER APPEARED TO LOSE CONFIDENCE OR BE BOTHERED BY THE PRESSURE. HE BEAT US."

Frank Orr, Hall of Fame hockey writer was at Boston Garden the afternoon that the Big Bad Bruins hit a wall named Dryden, and his dispatch in the *Toronto Star* summed it up in poetic style.

The defence rests: Dryden strikes a classic pose.

"It was early in yesterday's third period, Boston Bruins were in a power play situation, and they led with their ace," Orr wrote.

"Phil Esposito, their 76-goal shooter during the National Hockey League season, unloaded from the slot, the most productive move in history. Montreal Canadiens' elongated rookie goaltender, Ken Dryden, flicked up his arm, deflected the puck to the ice and fell on it.

"Out of sheer frustration, Esposito slammed his stick against the glass. The mighty Bruins were dead."

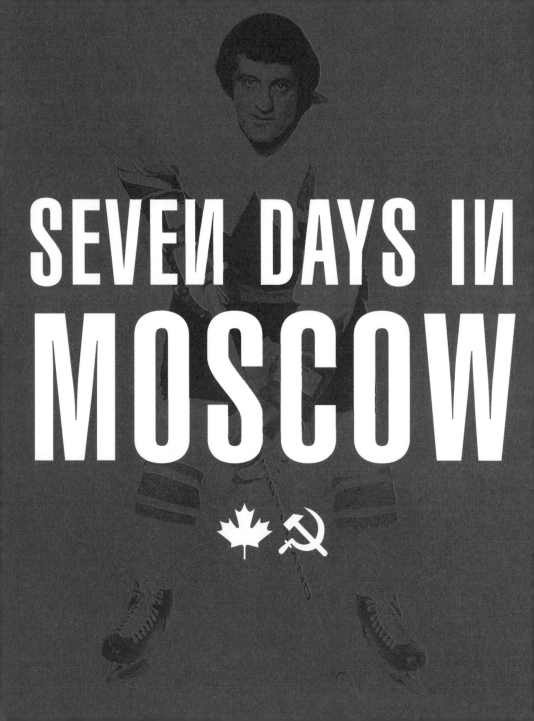

SEVEN DAYS IN
MOSCOW

TO RUSSIA WITH HATE

BY FRANK ORR

STRIP THE NUMBERS from Phil Esposito's 18-season NHL career, 717 goals, 873 assists, 1,590 points in 1,282 games, 100 of those goals game-winners. Delete his playoff excellence (61-76-137 point total in 130 games) and two Stanley Cup championships. Remove his awards: five scoring titles; twice the NHL's most valuable player; eight times the all-star centre; six selections to the first team.

Base his career summary on 27 days in September 1972, highlighted by a week in Moscow, and Esposito still tops the list of hockey's greatest heroes. In the fabled 1972 Summit Series between the national team of the old Soviet Union and Team Canada's collection of NHL stars, Esposito played hockey as well as anyone ever has and assumed a leadership role that the legendary generals of history might envy.

Paul Henderson, who scored the famous decisive series-winning goal after a big play by Esposito, said it best: "Phil was the 'all-everything' for our team in that series. He just kept going at them and took the rest of us with him."

The happenings of those 27 days were complex and multilayered, laden with politics and personalities, the stuff of great drama. Central in much of it was the big, outspoken, often sad-eyed Italian-Canadian from Sault Ste. Marie, Ontario, who went from often-maligned, frequently misunderstood

Captain Canada: Esposito dons the maple leaf.

NHL star to revered national hero.

The series had gained magnitude from its 18-year buildup after the Soviets, having played top-level hockey for only a few years, surprised a Canadian Senior B team from Toronto to win the world championship. Until 1972 Canadians endured the Soviet domination of world "amateur" hockey, confident that NHL players could destroy the upstarts from the Steppes. Thus, the first series between the Russians — to most North Americans they were "Russians," not "Soviets" — and a team of NHL stars was viewed as the time when the best of Canada's skaters would demonstrate easily where hockey's true power lay.

"All we knew was that we would have it easy because that's what those who thought they knew told us," Esposito said. "In training camp that summer, to get ready for the Russians, we had no idea [of] the huge hockey, political, jurisdictional, emotional wringer that we were heading for. We would breeze through a low-key training camp, play a couple of intrasquad games and whip the Russians.

"None of the smart guys in charge told us the bloody Russians had been preparing for the series for at least five years and had been training year-round.

"A few times in the late 1960s into the '70s, rumbles had the Russians ready to play the NHL's best but nothing came of it, I was told later on, because they didn't feel strong enough in all areas to compete. Goaltending lagged behind the rest of their hockey development and, despite big success in the world tournaments and Olympics, the Russians figured that NHL shooters would blow away their goalies.

"But when a kid named [Vladislav] Tretiak came along, they felt they had the man for the job. They sort of sneaked up on us with him."

Because Canada dropped out of the World Championship in 1970 in a dispute with the International Ice Hockey Federation over the use of professional players on the Canadian team, Tretiak and other talented young players made the U.S.S.R. national team almost unknown to North Americans. Pre-Summit scouting reports said the Soviet goaltending was weak, based on little information. Tretiak turned out to be a superb goaltender, a thorn in the NHL's side for the next dozen years.

The battle for control of Team Canada and the series was almost as competitive as the on-ice play. Hockey Canada, the umbrella organization created by government to oversee the country's international program, the NHL, whose players would stock the team, and the NHL Players' Association, a six-year-old group rapidly gaining strength under executive director Alan Eagleson, slugged it out to be in charge. In the end Eagleson took control, elbowing aside the politicians and bureaucrats.

Phil Esposito and his brother Tony, the excellent goalie for the Chicago Black Hawks, topped the list of the 35 players named to Team Canada, their selection automatic. But, as often happened in his career, controversy dogged Phil's involvement. The Esposito brothers had a summer hockey school in their hometown Sault Ste. Marie, and many youngsters had paid to receive instruction from the two NHL stars. When Phil said it would be difficult for him and Tony to attend Team Canada's training camp in mid-August, negative publicity was generated.

"I was portrayed as a villain, even a traitor to Canada, when I said it would be difficult to get out of the hockey school commitment to play," Esposito said. "Other players, like Walt Tkaczuk (New York Rangers), declined the invitation

PHIL ESPOSITO AND HIS BROTHER TONY, **THE EXCELLENT GOALIE FOR THE CHICAGO BLACK HAWKS, TOPPED THE LIST OF THE 35 PLAYERS NAMED TO TEAM CANADA, THEIR SELECTION AUTOMATIC.**

because of previous commitments, and they weren't scorned. We had many cancellations from our school because Tony and me weren't going to be there as advertised, and we had to refund the money."

The careers of the two great stars not on the roster, Bobby Hull and Bobby Orr, were intertwined with Esposito's. This often obscured Phil's value as a player, the assumption being that he had fed off their greatness. Their absence from the Summit provided Esposito's opening to take centre stage.

"It seemed my entire career people downgraded me, underestimated me, no matter what I accomplished," Esposito said. "The knockers said my success in Chicago was because I played with Hull, and when I got to Boston they said the team was great because of Orr. It was beneficial to me in a strange way, because it kept the heat off me."

The role of leader for Team Canada's series against the Soviets would have been a natural for Hull, whose blond good looks, magnetic personality and scoring feats had helped draw big crowds to games through the 1960s. Orr was the other obvious marquee name — his spectacular skill made him the league's biggest ticket-seller, especially in its new markets. But neither played in the Summit.

Just before the Canadian team was named, Hull signed a gigantic contract and defected from the Hawks, and the NHL, to the fledgling World Hockey Association. The NHL's czars, led by Chicago's Wirtz family, knew Hull's move had triggered a huge jump in hockey salaries. Their verdict was simple: If Hull plays, the other NHL players, under contract to us, do not. Even Canadian government intervention could not change the NHL's mind.

Orr had had knee injuries from the start of his NHL career in 1967 and in June 1972, after the Bruins won a second Cup in three seasons, he had a third operation on his left knee. He expected to be ready for the Summit Series and was named to the Team Canada roster. But his recovery was slow, the knee reducing him to spectator.

Team Canada's potential dipped considerably without Hull and Orr. Their absence also left a gap in another major area — leadership. Top young stars such as Bobby Clarke and Brad Park became team leaders later in their careers but were too young for the role in '72. Many older stars (Yvan Cournoyer, Rod Gilbert, Jean Ratelle, Serge Savard, Guy Lapointe, Frank Mahovlich, Bill White, Gary Bergman) were quiet men who just played and left the rah-rah to others.

"From the start of training camp, we lacked a player for the leader role, the guy in the centre of everything who spoke for the team and led by his example of total effort," said Team Canada general manager and head coach Harry Sinden. "We hoped that someone would step into that void, and seldom has an opportunity been seized the way Phil Esposito took over the leadership role with that team."

Esposito's emergence as Team Canada's go-to guy, both in his play and leadership/team-conscience role, evolved slowly. In training camp, as confidence about the series grew, leadership was not necessary, other than for tasks such as picking the best restaurants for dinner or the bar for the late-evening nightcap.

In the series' opener at the Montreal Forum, Canada's confidence seemed justified when Esposito scored after 30 seconds, Henderson in the seventh minute. But slowly the Canadian wheels fell off and the superbly conditioned and thoroughly drilled Soviets dominated in a stunning, 7-3 victory. "Never a shock in any of our lives like that night in Montreal," Esposito recalled. "We had the big start, then quickly ran out gas as they picked up the pace and we tried to catch them. None of what we had been told about them was correct. They were small, sure, but extraordinarily strong. They could hand out bodychecks with our best. And weak goaltending? Tretiak looked dandy to us.

"In that first game, we all realized they had two important things that we didn't — exceptional physical conditioning and great team play."

With a lineup change for Game 2 in Toronto, the Canadians played a grinding defensive game and, backed by Tony Esposito's brilliant goaltending, evened the series with a convincing 4-1 victory. Phil scored the first goal in the second period from the slot. In the third, with Canada in front 2-1, Esposito's bank pass off the boards launched Peter Mahovlich for a spectacular shorthanded goal, souring the Soviets' hopes of a comeback.

Before the third game in Winnipeg, grumbling was heard from the Team Canada players not used in the first two games, and from some who had played in the first game but sat out the next two. In Game 3 Team Canada twice had two-goal leads, 3-1 and 4-2, only to have the Soviets fight back for a 4-4 tie.

Scorn for Team Canada's struggles bubbled across the country, with editorial writers, radio and TV commentators and fans knocking the "shabby" effort after forecasts of a romp.

When the Canadians fell behind, 2-0, early in the fourth game at Vancouver, the first boos for the team were heard from the Pacific Coliseum crowd. Esposito seemed to play the entire third period, trying to pull Canada back from a 4-1 deficit. He set up two goals but in the end was unable to prevent a 5-3 loss.

In a postgame television interview with CTV sports director John Esaw,

Fenced in: Team Canada goalie Tony Esposito weathers a Soviet invasion as brother Phil heads for open ice.

Esposito delivered to the country a speech that became a turning point in the series, because it stamped him as Team Canada's leader. His eyes a picture of disbelief, his dark hair matted with sweat, Esposito berated those Canadians who had booed the team. This was just the tonic his beleaguered teammates needed.

"When Phil poured out his emotions, saying the things many of us were thinking, he became the undisputed leader of the team, the man who stood up and said what had to be said at the right time," said winger Henderson.

The team faced serious problems. There was continued division among the players, some of whom were disgruntled because of a lack of playing time, while others felt key players were not doing their jobs. Esposito's leadership, the first sense of which was established by his televised postgame speech in Vancouver, surfaced even more strongly in Stockholm. He met with Team Canada's executive director Eagleson and coach Sinden to state the players' case.

"A story started that when our wives met us in Moscow we would be in one hotel and they would be in another," Esposito said. "Then Eagle and Sinden suggested that we leave our wives at home. We had a meeting of the players and decided if the wives stayed home, we would join them quickly. When I told Eagleson that, he agreed and said just to have a go at it, even though it appeared we were in big trouble on the ice.

"During the camp in Canada the players got to know each other a little, but guys were going off to other places often to look after their business interests, like hockey schools, and there was no strong team feeling. Then we played four games in seven days, travelled in between, and that didn't help. In Stockholm, with no distractions, at least some all-for-one feeling started to grow."

When the Canadians reached Moscow, they found not only their wives and friends but close to 3,000 Canadian fans who had made the trip to see the games. This infusion of support, combined with several thousand telegrams from well-wishers back home, helped lift the players' spirits.

Moscow, however, was an ordeal. The Intourist Hotel, not far from Red Square, was by North American standards below mediocre — the rooms small, the food dreadful, especially the "mystery meat" of tourist fables: Was it beef, pork, chicken, goat, horse, political dissident? Food shipped from Canada, including a hefty load of steaks and beer, disappeared mysteriously.

That a dozen members of the team's 35-player roster saw little chance of playing in Moscow brought dissent to a head. When Vic Hadfield, a 50-goal scorer the previous season with the New York Rangers, discovered he wouldn't be dressed for the first game in Moscow, he asked team leader Eagleson to book a flight home for him and his wife. He was joined by youngsters Jocelyn Guevremont of the Vancouver Canucks and Richard Martin of the Buffalo

*Dream ticket: A stub from Game 8
of the Summit Series in Moscow.*

TEAM CANADA'S POTENTIAL DIPPED CONSIDERABLY WITHOUT HULL AND ORR. THEIR ABSENCE ALSO LEFT A GAP IN ANOTHER MAJOR AREA — LEADERSHIP. TOP YOUNG STARS SUCH AS BOBBY CLARKE AND BRAD PARK BECAME TEAM LEADERS LATER IN THEIR CAREERS BUT WERE TOO YOUNG FOR THE ROLE IN '72. MANY OLDER STARS (YVAN COURNOYER, ROD GILBERT, JEAN RATELLE, SERGE SAVARD, GUY LAPOINTE, FRANK MAHOVLICH, BILL WHITE, GARY BERGMAN) WERE QUIET MEN WHO JUST PLAYED AND LEFT THE RAH-RAH TO OTHERS.

Sabres and, after the first Moscow game, Buffalo's Gil Perreault, despite his having played well in that game.

"The core lineup and another group who stayed devoted to the effort, even though they had little chance of playing, became close quickly in Moscow," Esposito said. "The guys who left? Well, that was their choice. I had enough to worry about in guys wearing red-and-white uniforms."

The Canadian fans generated an incredible din in Moscow's musty old Luzhniki Arena as the visiting team started the game strongly, building a 4-1 lead early in the third period. But the Russians stormed back with four consecutive goals for a 5-4 victory and a 3-1-1 stranglehold on the series.

"What we learned in that game, although we realized it before, is that the Russians played the same no matter what the score was," Esposito said. "Ahead by four, down by three, they just kept coming, playing the same game. We got the lead, made some mistakes and they jumped on them.

"But it was a little strange after that game, the one that really put our asses in a vise, but no one on our team was down except my brother Tony, who thought he hadn't played very well in goal, although no one on the team agreed. We knew that after hard workouts in Sweden and Moscow our team was getting into good condition and could play our game.

"What was important to us was that when the game ended, those Canadian fans gave us a long, loud ovation, a big lift. Another key factor was that after five games we had started to figure out the Russian system of play, which had little variation in it. They stuck to the same strategy and we solved it, things like their criss-crossing in the neutral zone that we could break up when we got enough conditioning to skate with them. Our improvement really surfaced in the sixth game."

Team of the Century: Espo (front row, fourth from left) and the rest of Team Canada.

Ultimate road trip: Canadian fans cheer on their heroes in Moscow.

The two-referee system using officials from several countries was becoming a serious problem for the Canadians, accustomed to the crisp work of professional "zebras" in the NHL. Two West Germans, Franz Baader and Joseph Kompalla, were regarded as incompetent referees, even by European hockey observers, while Swede Uve Dahlberg and Rudy Bata from Czechoslovakia were much more efficient.

"In the NHL, usually the instigator of an exchange of fouls draws the penalty or, at worst, both the instigator and the retaliator," Esposito said. "It was a helluva change for us when a Russian very sneakily would spear us or throw a butt end, we'd give a whack in exchange, but we would get the only penalty."

Team Canada had a 3-1 lead early in the third period of the sixth game when Baader and Kompalla started to call "phantom" penalties against the Canadians for offences that no videotape had recorded. The Canadians received 31 minutes in penalties, the Russians four minutes. Included was a major to Esposito after he was flattened by large Russian defenceman Alexandr Ragulin. But brilliant penalty killing was critical in Canada's 3-2 victory.

"While we might not have had the offensive skills of the Russians — their great passing and skating — we were better than them defensively, smarter at analyzing their strategy and doing what we had to to break it up," Esposito said. "As the series went on, our defencemen, the position that always seems the slowest to come to a high level during the NHL season, got better and better. The Chicago pair, Pat Stapleton and Bill White, smart veterans, were effective in playing up the ice a little and cutting off the Russians' passing moves."

Esposito's two goals in the first period of Game 7 led to a 2-2 tie after

20 minutes and more strong penalty killing allowed the Canadians to escape five second-period penalties with no damage. An exchange of goals early in the third set the stage for Henderson's winner, a dazzling one-on-two rush from centre ice in which he bounced off a defenceman, regained control of the puck and, as he was falling to the ice, fired a shot that went under Tretiak's arm and into the net.

"After seven games and only a couple more days to go in that godawful place [Moscow], we could hardly wait to play the eighth game. The tactics they used on us to try and throw us off our game were incredible — telephone calls in the middle of the night, intercoms in our rooms that were supposed to be shut off blaring out at all hours, stealing our food, especially the steaks, and taking our beer. But looking back, I really think the bullshit they threw at us backfired on them. The crap just made us more determined to win the damned thing and to get the hell out of there."

Team Canada came close to leaving Moscow before the deciding game in the series. After the incompetent officiating of Kompalla and Baader in the sixth game, the Soviets agreed that neither ref would officiate again in the series. Dahlberg and Bata handled the seventh game reasonably well and the Canadians knew that the duo was the best they could hope for.

With the series hanging on a single game, the Soviets pulled a familiar trick from the Cold War days: They simply ignored agreements and promises. Originally, the Russians had the choice of officials in every other game (one, three, five, seven) while Canada would select the referees for the even-numbered ones. But that deal strangely vanished in Moscow.

Years later, a Russian hockey official admitted that when they realized the Canadians were upset by the work of Baader and, especially, Kompalla,

they wanted those officials for the concluding game. But when the Russians insisted that those two work the game, Team Canada threatened to abandon the series.

"Many figure we were posturing with talk of pulling out but, honestly, we were very serious about it," Esposito said. "Eagleson asked me what I thought and I felt it was the last straw in the long line of crap they dumped on us over there, all the off-ice stuff to try and upset us. You just can't imagine how frustrated we were, because we had gone through emotional hell and worked harder than any hockey team ever had to get back into the series. I told Eagle that if he figured we were getting screwed and that we should head home I was with him, and I was certain the other players would agree. If the game wasn't played, the Russkies would have lost a quarter million bucks in European TV money at a time they needed western loot."

Canada wanted Dahlberg and Bata to officiate but the Russians told Eagleson that Dahlberg was ill, minutes after Eagle and a healthy Dahlberg had talked. Dahlberg later admitted that the Russians threatened him with a ban from international hockey if he worked the eighth game.

The compromise was that each side named an official for the game. Team Canada picked Bata while the Russians, of course, selected Kompalla. "We were really pumped up as high as a team could get for that game, maybe too high, and our worst fears about the officiating were confirmed early when really lousy, cheap calls made us two men short for a minute and a half and the Russians scored," Esposito said. "Our guys were really on the edge and couldn't take any more crap."

Esposito scored the first goal for the Canadians in a 2-2 first period but the Russians went ahead, 5-3, after 40 minutes.

On the forecheck: Esposito tries to knock Soviet defenceman Alexander Gusev off the puck.

"I have very vivid memories of the calm feeling in the dressing room before the third period, the quiet confidence that we weren't out of it, even though they had a rather large two-goal lead," Esposito said. "The big target was to not let them get ahead by another goal, by taking chances in trying to score ourselves."

Esposito's extraordinary play in the final period remains etched in the minds of anyone who watched it, the players and team officials, the Canadian fans in Luzhniki and the gigantic television audience back home. Estimates, from an era when precise playing time was not recorded, have him on the ice for 14 of the final period's 20 minutes.

"I was lucky to get the goal that I consider perhaps the most important one in the series because it cut their lead to one," he said. "I was in the slot, Pete Mahovlich sent me a pass that went high, I knocked it to the ice and put it in the net.

"Not long after that goal, an unusual thing happened that I feel influenced the outcome. [New York Ranger] Rod Gilbert, who had become an effective player for us, got into a real fist fight with a Russian [Evgeny Mishakov]. Gilbert is not a fighter by any assessment but he had enough stick shit from the Russian guy, dropped the gloves and went after him. That gave us all a lift, the idea that we were still full of fight and very much alive in the game.

"We played a great period of hockey when we needed it most. We were strong defensively, patient on the attack to wait for some good chances [a 14-5 third-period edge in shots on goal], confident we could outplay them in the final 10 minutes if we had a chance."

Esposito did the spadework on the tying goal, too, fighting off two defenders to deliver a shot that Tretiak stopped only to have Yvan

Top: Teams line up for pre-game ceremonies at Moscow's Luzhniki Arena. Bottom: Scoreboard early in third period of Game 8, before Canada's comeback.

Cournoyer tap in the rebound at 12.56.

Just when it appeared that the series would end in a 3-3-2 deadlock — the Russians said they would claim victory because they had outscored Team Canada 32-30 — the Canadians produced "the goal heard around the world" in the final minute of play.

Esposito stayed on the ice at the end of a long shift, the puck in the Russian zone, and a tired winger, Cournoyer, turned back into the play instead of going to the bench. Henderson yelled for Pete Mahovlich to come off and jumped on in time to create history.

"Both Yvan and me stayed on the ice when we should have got off and when the Russians simply tried to clear the puck from their zone, Cournoyer got it," said Esposito, describing the slow-motion replay of the shift, still etched in his mind.

"Henderson was full tilt down the wing and Cournoyer tried to pass to Paul. The pass went behind Henderson and when he reached back for it he was dumped to the ice by a Russian and slid to the end boards. I headed for it with three Russians between me and the puck and I figured they would bang it out of their zone. But the guy with it couldn't control it and the puck came to me in the faceoff circle. Paul had regained his feet and was moved to the front of the net, all alone with Tretiak. I shot. Tretiak stopped it. Henderson got the rebound and shot. Tretiak stopped that, but Paul shot in the rebound." The words of broadcast legend Foster Hewitt — "Henderson has scored for Canada" — are the most famous in Canadian hockey history.

Team Canada head coach Harry Sinden offered the best summation of Esposito's play: "Quite simply, Phil was not going to let us lose that game and what he did was incredible. Even 20 and more years later, in thinking and looking back on that series and especially that eighth game, he dominated the picture. Every time we needed a big play he delivered it, and not just offensively. He was exceptional in a defensive role, too, killing penalties and working his butt off in our end of the ice.

"Cripes, in that game, Ken Dryden was down after making a save and a Russian had an open net to shoot at. Esposito slid through the crease on his knees and stopped the shot to save a goal and likely the game."

Reflecting on the series years later, Boris Mikhailov, a revered figure in Russian hockey but a lifelong critic of Canadian tactics, praised Esposito.

"Canada had many good players in that series, but the one man who had more to do with beating us than anyone was Phil Esposito," Mikhailov said.

On reflection, Esposito still has mixed emotions about the Summit.

"We probably shouldn't have played that series because we had too much to lose, very little to gain," he said. "All in all, it wasn't a pleasant experience for me. We didn't get in shape until Moscow, and when we did we became a team that no one could beat. I feel certain that if we had played 10 more games in Moscow, we would have won them all.

"But even taking all that into consideration and that it was like going through hell, I wouldn't have missed it for the world. In the end, no matter how a lot of smart people have said it wasn't that way, it came down to our society against theirs, like in a war."

Frank Orr was an NHL *beat writer for the* Toronto Star *during the famed 1972 Summit Series.*

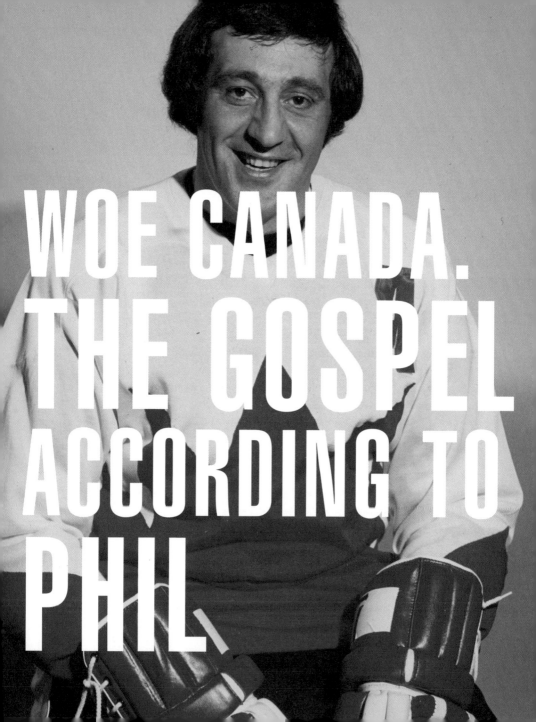

VEXED IN VANCOUVER
BY CRAIG MacINNIS

IT WAS THE SPEECH that galvanized a nation and changed the course of hockey history.

Wait. Check that. "Speech" isn't quite the right term for what transpired the night of September 8, 1972, when Phil Esposito found himself staring into the abyss at Vancouver's Pacific Coliseum, boos raining down on him from fair-weather fans who had just watched their hockey heroes fall 5-3 to the Soviets in Game 4 of the Summit Series.

The devastating loss, in which Canada had resorted to cheap shots while the Soviets danced around them with maddening ease, left the series 2-1-1 in Russia's favour as it headed to Moscow for Game 5. How were we ever going to win there if we couldn't win here?

Canada looked beaten and outclassed in a game that was as much political allegory as athletic contest — a clash of systems that was supposed to prove our dominance over the "red menace" but was only proving how deluded we'd been in our judgements. If our hockey team couldn't beat theirs, what else did we need to know? Was there even a God?

The usually mild Canadian temperament gave way to hostility, directed at the easiest available target — the players who weren't upholding the country's smug assumptions about its invincibility on ice.

Espo's comments to CTV interviewer Johnny Esaw — triggered because Espo had won the dubious distinction of being Canada's "star of the game" — more closely resembled an unrehearsed plea than a strategic address to the nation, but he saw his opening and took it.

"People across Canada, we tried, we gave it our best," a fed-up Espo told Esaw. "To the people that boo us, all of us guys are really disheartened and we're disillusioned and we're disappointed in some of the people. We cannot believe the bad press we've got, the booing we've gotten in our own building ...

"I'm really disappointed," he continued. "I am completely disappointed. I cannot believe it. Some of our guys are really, really down in the dumps. We know. We're trying, but hell, we're doing the best we can. They've got a good team and let's face facts. It doesn't mean we're not giving it our 150 percent, because we certainly are."

You can't be a Canadian of a certain age and not remember the sting of Espo's heartfelt, stream-of-consciousness masterpiece. His words are seared into our collective memory, like the lyrics to "O Canada," like Pierre Trudeau's "Just watch me!" pledge during the FLQ crisis.

None of it was planned. "Honest to God, that just came out," Espo said years later in the documentary "Summit on Ice". "I never saw that [the tape of his televised outburst] until 1981 or '82. People used to tell me about it when I'd travel around Canada, but I'd never seen or heard what I really said."

Viewed more than 30 years later, his words and gestures from that night — the breathless delivery, the slumped shoulders, the sheen of game sweat on his furrowed brow — still pack a surprising emotional wallop.

Hindsight is everything. We can savour the fact that his plea meant

"PEOPLE ACROSS CANADA, WE TRIED, WE GAVE IT OUR BEST. TO THE PEOPLE THAT BOO US, ALL OF US GUYS ARE REALLY DISHEART- ENED AND WE'RE DISILLUSIONED AND WE'RE DISAPPOINTED IN SOME OF THE PEOPLE. WE CANNOT BELIEVE THE BAD PRESS WE'VE GOT, THE BOOING WE'VE GOTTEN IN OUR OWN BUILDING ...

"I'M REALLY DISAPPOINTED.

I AM COMPLETELY DISAPPOINTED. I CANNOT BELIEVE IT. SOME OF OUR GUYS ARE REALLY, REALLY DOWN IN THE DUMPS. WE KNOW. WE'RE TRYING, BUT HELL, WE'RE DOING THE BEST WE CAN. THEY'VE GOT A GOOD TEAM AND LET'S FACE FACTS. IT DOESN'T MEAN WE'RE NOT GIVING IT OUR 150 PERCENT, BECAUSE WE CERTAINLY ARE."

something to the series and the way things turned out for Canada. We can also marvel at the courage it must have taken to stand up and look the country in the eye, instead of just shuffling off to the dressing room and smashing his stick over a garbage can.

"Every one of us guys — 35 guys — that came out and played for Team Canada, we did it because we love our country and not for any other reason," he said in another memorable passage from his ice-level plea.

"They can throw the money for the [players'] pension fund out the window and they can throw everything they want out the window. We came because we love Canada, and even though we play in the United States and we earn money in the United States, Canada is still our home and that's the only reason we come and I don't think it's fair that we should be booed."

Esaw, already a famous broadcaster before 1972, became more famous after Espo's tirade. Esaw would become known as the guy who coaxed the greatest interview ever from a hockey player departing the ice.

"I kept going with Phil as long as he wanted to talk," Esaw recalled years later. "In the mood that he was in, I was going to let him talk because I knew I had a classic."

For his part, Espo remembered Esaw "just letting [the interview] go," and recalled a few other salient details: "I remember being so frustrated that I almost was on the verge of swearing two or three times. It was hot, and there were a couple of people up in the stands who were throwing things at me and they were yelling obscenities at me."

In "Summit On Ice", Esaw ventures that Esposito "got the whole country to suddenly examine themselves, to understand what they were doing to these players, players who had been working so tremendously hard."

In the next day's papers Esposito repeated the remarks he had made for television, but quickly added that he would play for Canada again if asked. "In a minute, tomorrow. I love this country."

Not all of his teammates were so quick to forgive. In a Toronto *Globe and Mail* article by Dick Beddoes, Team Canada defenceman Brad Park was quoted as saying, "Next year I won't be back if a similar series is promoted against Russia. When the country boos you for something you're doing for your country, there's more important things to do. My wife has just had a baby, and spending time with them is more important."

ACROSS THE COUNTRY, THOUGH, ESPO'S WORDS BECAME A RALLYING CRY FOR CANADIANS DETERMINED TO CHEER ON THEIR BATTERED TEAM AS IT HEADED TO THE UNFRIENDLY CONFINES OF MOSCOW'S LUZHNIKI ARENA IN LENIN SPORTS PALACE.

"After I talked on TV, I got 10 to 15 long-distance calls in the dressing room," Espo told the *Globe and Mail*. "I got them from coast to coast and they were all favourable. Mrs. Dorothy Long phoned from Halifax. A Rev. Steele called from Jasper, Alberta. Wally Hergesheimer — remember when he played? — phoned to say 'keep punching.' They all said we're in this as a country, and ought to pull together as a country." [Hergesheimer, a Winnipegger, was a star in the early 1950s with the New York Rangers.]

That we eventually did just that — pulled together as one unified, hockey-crazed nation of righteous, proud Canadians, willing to go the distance with this team that had brought us to the brink, willing to fall alongside them in the decisive eighth game if fate decreed a loss — might be the greatest communal achievement known to Canadians of the postwar era.

Without Espo setting the tone amid the doubters and boo-birds in Vancouver that bitter September night, it's hard to imagine that any of it would have happened.

Craig MacInnis was a 16-year-old hockey fanatic, fighting back tears in front of his parents' TV set in St. Catharines, Ontario, when the Soviets beat Canada in Game 4.

A CONVERT TO THE CHURCH OF ESPOSITO

LARGE AND IN CHARGE

BY DOUG HEROD

GROWING UP IN THE 1960s, I had some pretty definite ideas on the skills required to be a great player. Phil Esposito didn't have them. He lacked the power of Bobby Hull, the puck-handling wizardry of Stan Mikita, the elegance and intelligence of Jean Beliveau, the craftiness and toughness of Gordie Howe.

Not that I wasted a lot of time weighing the merits of Esposito against other stars. He was a low-profile plugger for the offensively talented Chicago Black Hawks. True, he had twice finished among the Top 10 scorers in the six-team NHL, a not inconsiderable accomplishment. But he was pretty much off the radar screen for casual followers of the Hawks, dominated as they were by the likes of Hull and Mikita. Besides, who couldn't pick up a few garbage goals and points playing on the same line as the Golden Jet?

Esposito's value took a hit in the 1966–67 Stanley Cup semifinals when the heavily favoured Hawks were beaten by the Toronto Maple Leafs. The second-line centre, held pointless during the series, could hardly be held responsible for the shocking defeat. But he was a convenient scapegoat for management, which felt compelled to do something short of trading some of their real stars. Boy, they must have been mad at him! He was traded to the Boston Bruins, who, after years of practice, had their imitation of a doormat down pat.

But Esposito was quickly earning a reputation as a guy who could fall in a bucket of manure and come out smelling like a rose. First, he graduates to the bigs and lands a job setting up the league's most prolific goal scorer in Hull. Next, he gets traded to Boston just as Bobby Orr goes from blue-chip prospect to bona fide superstar.

Let's see, Orr gets the puck behind the net, dodges a couple of forwards on his way past the blue line, gathers speed at centre, feints toward the middle as he crosses the other blue line, slips the puck between a defenceman's skates, dekes the goalie to one side and then slides the puck over to Esposito, who knocks it into the deserted net. Nice work if you can get it. But that's okay. Somebody had to benefit from Orr's brilliance. Why not some lunch-bucket type who had toiled in relative anonymity throughout his young career? And his efforts were helping lift the Bruins to respectability. After years of seeing the same teams in the playoffs, it was refreshing to have Boston join the battle. But things soon turned sour. I mean, it was one thing for a johnny-come-lately to emerge as a league scoring leader, quite another for him to challenge scoring records. Who did he think he was, anyway?

TO ARMCHAIR ATHLETES, ESPOSITO HAD FEW REDEEMING QUALITIES. HE SEEMED SLOW, DIDN'T POSSESS A PARTICULARLY HARD SHOT, WAS FOREVER WHINING AND LETTING OTHER PEOPLE FIGHT HIS FIGHTS.

His claim to fame was a big ass that was hard to move from in front of the net. Not exactly a model to emulate on the rinks and road hockey venues of the nation. "He shoots, it's off my butt, I score! Just like Espo!"

And Esposito did score goals. Lots of them. Forty-nine one year, followed by 54. Then 76. Egads, 76! What an insult to the truly great

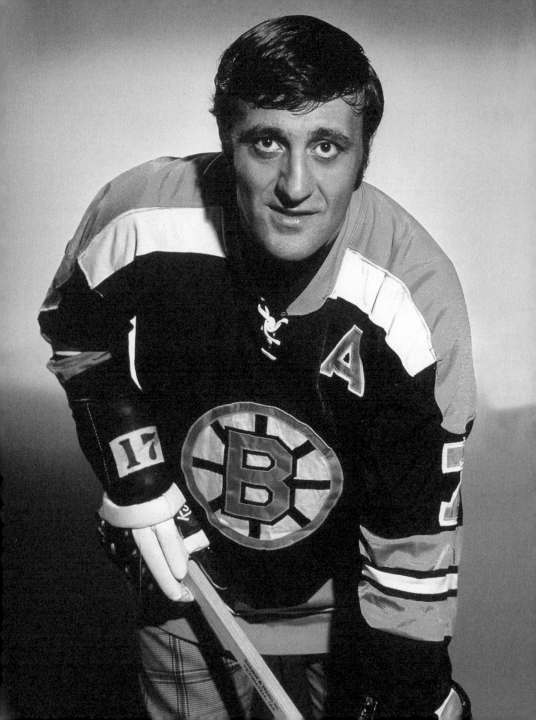

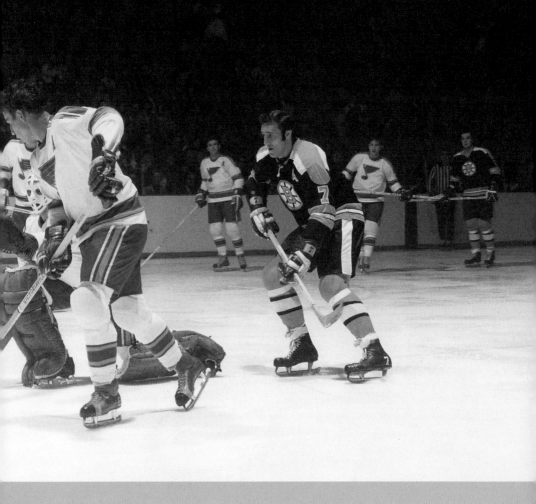

THE BRUINS WERE THE NOUVEAU RICHE OF HOCKEY AND NOBODY REPRESENTED THEIR QUESTIONABLE PEDIGREE BETTER THAN ESPOSITO.

players of the era. An absolute disgrace.

Someone like Esposito, who couldn't hold a candle to icons like Hull, Howe and Mikita, now held the league's goal-scoring record. It was embarrassing, or at least that's how I remember feeling at the time.

Take Orr away or have Esposito play against real teams instead of pretenders from Pittsburgh and Oakland and see how many goals he'd get then.

Adding to my resentment of Esposito was that the team he played for had lost its novelty status as a contending team. Boston was brash, dirty and played before obnoxious, beer-swigging louts disguised as fans. Give me the distinguished manner of the champion Canadian-based teams and their civil supporters any day.

The Bruins were the nouveau riche of hockey and nobody represented their questionable pedigree better than Esposito. All he'd do was park in front of the net while big lugs like Ken Hodge and Wayne Cashman dug the puck out of the corners for him. Or he waited for Orr to set him up. Or he just hung around the crease knocking in rebounds with his long reach.

Did this guy ever score a goal from more than 15 feet out? The Bruins' combination of Orr, supporting talent and team thuggery won them Cups in 1970 and 1972. But was anything sweeter than seeing this bunch of swaggering no-goodniks get upset by Montreal in 1971, the very year Esposito shattered Hull's record by scoring 76 goals? The hockey gods had exacted revenge.

Then along came the 1972 Canada-Soviet Union Summit Series, where Esposito would play Orr-less. While Orr's absence caused some to expect a drop in Esposito's production, that wasn't the case in the first few games. He accumulated his usual share of points. Not that anyone noticed,

Big bad Bruin: Esposito heads
to the slot against the Blues.

of course. Canadians were too upset over the pathetic efforts of their team to dwell on individual performances. Canada was down two games to one with another tied after the completion of the fourth match in Vancouver and looked bedraggled, bewitched and brutal doing it. *B-o-o-o-o-o-o-o-o!* Up to a postgame microphone stepped the heretofore underappreciated Phil Esposito. As any Canadian hockey fan of a certain vintage knows, Esposito, heart on his sleeve, spontaneously vented frustration, disappointment and incredulity to a soon-to-be sheepish nation. Dripping sweat, he told of the disbelief and shame his teammates felt at the disdain Canadians were displaying toward them.We're all proud Canadians, he said of his colleagues. We gladly took time off from our short summer to represent our country. We're playing our guts out to win against what has turned out be a very good Soviet team. And yet, said a distraught Esposito, we're being booed. In Canada. By Canadians. Man, it hurts. It really, really hurts.

Phil, we're sorry! Forgive us! It's just that world hockey supremacy is kinda what a lot of us live for. So, okay, just go over to the Soviet Union and try your darndest.

The rest, as those of us not afraid to cheapen the term say, is history. Canada took three out of four games in Moscow and proved, if not beyond a reasonable doubt, at least on a balance of probabilities, that it was the greatest hockey nation in the world. And Esposito was the undisputed captain.

Paul Henderson was rightly crowned hockey hero after his winning goal in the final game, but it was Esposito who, through will and determination, seemingly carried the team to victory. Did I only say will and determination? How about skill, too? Yes, skill. It turns out Esposito wasn't some slow-footed trash collector who just picked up garbage around the net. He was an immensely strong athlete and well-balanced skater, able to fend off two or three opponents at a time while stationed in key scoring positions.

In 1971, an NHL coaches' poll had voted Espo not only "most dangerous near the goal" but "best stickhandler," quite a feat in a league that included Stan Mikita, Gordie Howe and Jean Beliveau.

Not only did Espo's long reach enable him to get to seemingly stray pucks, but he was then able to make deft moves in an area the size of a phone booth.

Or, once he had gained possession of the puck, he could simply fire off a quick shot with deadly accuracy past the most agile of goalies. During the Summit Series, he also brought into focus what had previously been, for most armchair athletes, a rather fuzzy concept — team leader. Yeah, sure, we had always heard and read about how so-and-so and what's-his-name showed real leadership for their teams, but belief in these roles always required leaps of faith.

IT WAS HARD TO DETECT EXACTLY HOW THESE LABELS WERE EARNED. FOR ALL WE KNEW, THE TERM WAS THRUST UPON THOSE WHO ARRANGED POSTGAME PUB CRAWLS. JUST GIVE US THE GUY WHO SCORED A LOT OF GOALS. HE WAS THE MAN. **BUT ESPOSITO CLEARLY DEMONSTRATED ON A HIGHLY VISIBLE STAGE WHAT LEADERSHIP WAS ALL ABOUT.**

Throughout the series he could be seen rallying his teammates, playing with the crowd, working the refs, backchecking, forechecking, driving the net, killing penalties, pivoting the power play, playing every shift as if it was his last. He even called a football huddle in the dying moments of the last

Marquis de Blade: Espo shows off his curve.

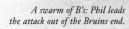

*A swarm of B's: Phil leads
the attack out of the Bruins end.*

game! The man was large and in charge. Esposito, a player whose elevated place in the game had always been somewhat suspect despite setting scoring records and winning Stanley Cups, had finally climbed to the top of the hockey charts in Canada.

Ironically, once he had achieved such exalted status he was never able to match his past glories. Don't get me wrong: He still had the touch. In the three seasons following the Summit Series he scored 55, 68 and 61 goals. He also won the most valuable player award in 1973–74. But it's a team game, right? And the talent-laden Bruins of the early 1970s never won another Stanley Cup. Hell, the Orr/Esposito squad made it to only one other final, losing to the Philadelphia Flyers in 1974. An expansion team, for crying out loud!

Sorry. Didn't mean to boo you, Phil. I'm a convert. You were a great player.

Doug Herod is a columnist for the St. Catharines Standard, *in the city where Espo played his final season of junior with the Teepees.*

Phil or Frank?: Espo, showing an uncanny resemblance to Leaf great Frank Mahovlich.

TRADER PHIL TAKES MANHATTAN

BY **ROB ADLER**

THE HAVOC PHIL ESPOSITO CREATED while working the slot in front of NHL goaltenders was merely a rehearsal for the chaos he caused when he moved to the front office. You thought he was prolific in his 76-goal season in Boston? That's nothing. Check out the numbers he put up as general manager of the New York Rangers. Now that was an awe-inspiring performance. When his career as a player ended after the 1980–81 season, Espo spent five years as an analyst on Rangers telecasts, which some might consider a dubious apprenticeship for his next gig — GM of the Blueshirts. He was hired in July 1986 and wasted no time moving the pieces around.

During his three seasons as general manager and occasional head coach Esposito earned the sobriquet "Trader Phil," and not by accident. In that span, Espo engineered a staggering 43 trades in which 40 players and eight draft choices moved to Manhattan while 49 bodies and four draft picks headed out of town. How busy was Trader Phil? Try this on for size — the Vancouver Canucks made only three trades more in the entire decade, proof that Phil, post-career, was more intent than ever on setting records.

One New York writer summed up his tenure this way: "Is he Trader Phil or just Fickle Phil?" Espo was never satisfied. One trade led to another, which led to another, which led to more trades to "complete" the team's

Boss man: Espo as Rangers' GM.

ever-changing picture.

New Jersey's Pat Burns, whose tour of duty through the Original Six franchises includes coaching stops in Montreal, Toronto and Boston, once said of Espo: "Why do GMs always want to coach? I could never work for a guy like that."

Working? Who said anything about working? Coaches scarcely had time to find an apartment, much less run a practice down at the rink, before they were gone. In all, there were five bench bosses (including Espo himself) during Trader Phil's busy tenure at Madison Square Garden.

He didn't lose the urge to swap when he became GM of the expansion Tampa Bay Lightning, either. In his six seasons in that job he engineered 63 moves, shipping out 56 players and 24 draft choices in exchange for 60 players and 26 draft picks. In hockey circles, Esposito's acumen as a dealer drew typically mixed reviews, everything from "He's crazy!" to "Wow, that Phil, sly as a fox." But with the Rangers appearing in only two playoff games in his three-year term, most judged Espo more nutty than shrewd.

Espo, for his part, assured us that his pell-mell approach to general managing was all part of an intricate blueprint for success. Just don't ask him to explain it.

"Impulsive, yes. But impatient, no," Espo said of his management style. "I have a master plan, contrary to what some people like to say. And I'm not crazy, contrary to what some people like to think."

When he left the Rangers even Espo conceded, "In the end, I was nowhere close to the team I wanted." Few clubs have spent as much time fearing telephone calls or a summons to the GM's office as the Rangers did during Esposito's tenure. Players joked that they never had to pack their bags for a road trip because they already had their luggage by the door. Of receiving a call at 7:30 a.m. from Espo, former Ranger Brian Lawton quipped, "I knew it wasn't to wish me a Merry Christmas." Being a New York Ranger during the Espo years meant taking to heart the old adage, "Don't buy any green bananas" — you'll only leave town before they ripen.

Ranger fans learned that the word "never" had an entirely different application for Phil. For Phil, "never" could be the minutes ticking by 'til breakfast. Case in point: The most popular Ranger of the era was the Blueshirts' hardworking winger, Don Maloney. Espo swore that Maloney was one horse he "would never trade." But before you could say, "Hey, what's the weather like in Connecticut?" Maloney was on his way to Hartford. Shortly after the trade, Espo said mournfully, "Giving up Don Maloney bothers me tremendously. There is no doubt that this is the toughest trade I've ever made. Sometimes this job just stinks."

Maloney had mixed emotions about the deal. "It hasn't been the greatest day for me, but I could be in Armenia. But on the other hand, it's nice to go where you're wanted. As soon I heard about it, I said 'Goodbye New York, hello Hartford!'"

Maybe the worst deal Esposito made for the Rangers was landing forward Bob Carpenter three years after Carpenter notched 53 goals for the Washington Capitals. To acquire Carpenter and the Caps' second-round pick in the 1989 entry draft, the Rangers surrendered their leading scorer from the previous season, Mike Ridley, along with Kelly Miller and Bob Crawford. The defensively sound Ridley had seven 20-goal-plus seasons in Washington, while Miller toiled for 13 solid campaigns.

Meanwhile, the Rangers ended up using their draft pick to select Jason

IN FLORIDA, ESPO SET HOCKEY ON ITS EAR WHEN HE INVITED A 20-YEAR-OLD WOMAN NAMED MANON RHEAUME, WHO HAD PLAYED MEN'S JUNIOR HOCKEY WITH THE TROIS RIVIERES DRAVEURS IN QUEBEC, TO TRAINING CAMP IN THE FALL OF 1992. BEFORE RHEAUME MADE IT ONTO THE ICE, ESPO INELEGANTLY BUT TRUTHFULLY OPINED: "I'D BE A LIAR IF I SAID I WASN'T USING IT FOR THE PUBLICITY."

Profosky, who promptly disappeared into the minor pro woodwork. Carpenter remained a Ranger for a scant 28 games, firing two goals. He was peddled to the Los Angeles Kings for past-his-prime, 37-year-old legend Marcel Dionne, who closed out his illustrious career with two solid if unexceptional seasons in New York.

After his coffee in New York, Carpenter was famously retooled into a durable defensive forward who logged another dozen NHL campaigns, including a valuable stint with the tight-checking 1995 Stanley Cup champion New Jersey Devils.

Another of Espo's career-defining swaps was for the feisty and diminutive bench boss Michel Bergeron, "Le Petit Tigre," whom the Rangers acquired from the Quebec Nordiques in 1987, in a rare deal involving a coach. As compensation for Bergeron, the Rangers sent their first-round pick, fifth overall, to the Nords. The Espo-Bergeron relationship was tempestuous from the start. Two games from the end of Bergeron's second season, Esposito fired him.

"We had so many injuries this year, but I am proud of these guys," Bergeron said on his way out the door. "If he gets the glory, it's because the boys are playing well and that's all I care about. I like these players.

"I'll shoulder the blame, that's the way the game is, but I don't understand it and I don't think it's a fair call. I've coached nine years in this league and my record is over .500 because the players know I always tell them the truth. This is not the truth ... again."

Espo handled the team himself for the remaining two games, then was canned six weeks after the end of the season, closing out his run on Broadway. History tells us that the Bergeron deal was a particularly nasty bone-in-the-throat for Rangers fans. With that draft pick Esposito could have claimed

Manon Rheaume: First woman to play goal in an NHL contest.

Jeremy Roenick, Rod Brind'Amour or Teemu Selanne, all of whom were available when the fifth pick was called. (In a dubious parlay, the Nordiques, using their chit from the Rangers, ended up taking Daniel Dore with the fifth pick. He played all of 17 games in the NHL.)

Having built his reputation in New York, Espo was well prepared for his headline-grabbing stint with the Tampa Bay Lightning, a Keystone Kops-style adventure in which he employed a female goaltender during a preseason game and somehow managed never to meet Takashi Okubo, the majority owner of the Japanese group that controlled the franchise. Espo, always a master of candour, once conceded that he didn't know who Okubo was until 1993. That was three years after Okubo had became owner of the Lightning.

In Florida, Espo set hockey on its ear when he invited a 20-year-old woman named Manon Rheaume, who had played men's junior hockey with the Trois Rivieres Draveurs in Quebec, to training camp in the fall of 1992. Before Rheaume made it onto the ice, Espo inelegantly but truthfully opined, "I'd be a liar if I said I wasn't using it for the publicity. The fact is, if I could put a horse in net — if it could stand on skates and stop the puck — I'd do it." Espo's naysayers waited with mounting terror, fearing an imminent announcement that Mr. Ed had cracked the Lightning roster and would be starting at centre, forming a line with Secretariat and Seattle Slew. Rheaume, to her credit, went out and made history by tending goal in the first period of a preseason game against the St. Louis Blues, a not-bad performance in which she surrendered two goals on nine shots.

Espo, for his part, eventually found some nice things to say about his new recruit. "Manon does have hockey talent," he told reporters. "There is no doubt about it in my mind. She's got hockey sense and hockey talent and guts.

Those three make for a hockey player."

The female puck-stopper won the hearts of women players everywhere, who cheered her pioneering efforts as the first female to appear in an NHL contest. Red-blooded males seemed impressed that a "babe" had crashed hockey's gender barrier. While the stunt was just that — a bid to create publicity for an attention-starved franchise — the Rheaume chapter couldn't help but raise the bar for women in hockey, which is also part of Esposito's legacy. Rheaume eventually became famous not only for her brief stay in The Show but as one of the netminders for Canada's national women's team. By the end of the '90s, both the U.S. and Canada had built strong distaff rosters, fighting each other for gold at the Nagano and Salt Lake City Winter Olympics.

Espo wasn't thinking about women's suffrage when he gave Rheaume her start against the Blues, but he definitely succeeded in causing one of the biggest media-hype storms the game has known — another entry in his bulging record book of firsts.

Rob Adler won Emmy Awards in 2001 and 2002 for his work as a researcher and interviewer for the American sports network ESPN. He lives in Hartford, Connecticut.

WHAT THEY SAID
QUOTABLE QUOTES ON PHIL ESPOSITO

"Our greatest challenge will be finding a way to control Esposito in front of the net."
— Soviet co-coach Vsevolod Bobrov, before the 1972 Canada-Soviet series

"What he gave to the Canadian cause was immense. He handled almost every emergency that arose and was the middleman on two separate forward lines."
— sportswriter Jim Proudfoot, paying tribute to Espo's stellar performance for Team Canada

"Phil isn't any different here than with the Bruins. It's just that now people are noticing."
— goalie and teammate Eddie Johnston, commenting on Espo's high profile with Canadian hockey fans during the '72 Soviet series

"I lost my right arm, my right arm."
— former Chicago linemate Bobby Hull, bemoaning Espo's trade to the Bruins

"Phil looks at the funny side of things, and when he starts laughing, soon everybody's laughing."

— Bruins assistant trainer John Foristall

"I can go full speed for only a minute. A big man like Esposito figures to have more stamina: he can go two minutes at full speed. And it's near the end of shifts, when other people are tired and a big man isn't, that a lot of goals are scored."

— Chicago star Stan Mikita, explaining Espo's size advantage

"He has a wide stance and keeps his balance well. I don't think I have ever seen anyone who can move so well through traffic."

— Bruins coach Tom Johnson, on the immovable object known as Espo

"He's got such long arms, he can reach out with his stick and get a pass 10 or 15 feet away from him."

— Bobby Orr, on Espo's legendary reach

"He is the best stickhandler I have ever seen."

— Bruins teammate Ted Green, on Phil's ability to hang onto the puck

"He has an almost fantastic ability to slow the game down. So many goals are missed because the forwards are going too fast. He increases the percentage of scoring by slowing the game down."

— Vancouver coach Hal Laycoe, on Espo's unique ice tempo

"Cash and I, we tell Phil, 'Get your tail into that slot and start shooting.'"

— Bruin Ken Hodge, describing the advice he and Wayne Cashman offered to their high-scoring linemate

"His casual, almost careless way reminds me of a younger Dean Martin. A gold watchband gleams from one wrist, a thick gold bracelet from the other, and his silver cufflinks flash in the light of a nearby lamp. I can imagine him suddenly bursting out with 'That's Amore.'"

— writer John Devaney commenting on Espo's flashy attire

"Phil would come over to me and say, 'Vad, what the hell are we doing here? We don't belong here.' He could never get accustomed to being a New York Ranger."
— teammate Carol Vadnais, who went from Boston to New York with Espo in the November 1975 trade

"He's a five-time scoring champion. Can you imagine that? If you win it once you're lucky."
— young Ranger Nick Fotiu, marvelling at new teammate Espo's stats

"Ah, Phil. We are good friends now. But I think he was mistaken about our government bugging Canadians' hotel rooms. No one was interested in their secrets. After all, they were hockey players, not spies."
— Soviet defenceman Aleksandr Ragulin denies Esposito's claims of KGB tampering during the '72 series

PHIL ESPOSITO

YEAR	TEAM	GP	G	A	PTS	PIM
1963–64	Chicago Black Hawks	27	03	02	05	02
1964–65	Chicago Black Hawks	70	23	32	55	44
1965–66	Chicago Black Hawks	69	27	26	53	49
1966–67	Chicago Black Hawks	69	21	40	61	40
1967–68	Boston Bruins	74	35	49	84	21
1968–69	Boston Bruins	74	49	77	126	79
1969–70	Boston Bruins	76	43	56	99	50
1970–71	Boston Bruins	78	76	76	152	71
1971–72	Boston Bruins	76	66	67	133	76
1972–73	Boston Bruins	78	55	75	130	87
1973v74	Boston Bruins	78	68	77	145	58
1974–75	Boston Bruins	79	61	66	127	62
1975–76	Boston Bruins	12	06	10	16	08
	New York Rangers	62	29	38	67	28
1976–77	New York Rangers	80	34	46	80	52
1977–78	New York Rangers	79	38	43	81	53
1978–79	New York Rangers	80	42	36	78	14
1979–80	New York Rangers	80	34	44	78	73
1980–81	New York Rangers	41	07	13	20	20
TOTALS		1282	717	873	1590	887
PLAYOFF TOTALS		130	61	76	137	137

YEAR	TOURNAMENT	GP	G	A	PTS	PIM
1972	Summit Series	08	07	06	13	15
1976–77	Canada Cup	07	04	03	07	00

CAREER FACTS AND HIGHLIGHTS

BORN FEBRUARY 20, 1942, IN SAULT STE. MARIE, ONTARIO. CENTRE, SHOOTS LEFT, 6'1", 205 LBS.

OLDER BROTHER OF NHL GOALTENDING GREAT TONY ESPOSITO, BORN APRIL 23, 1943

AFTER BEING CUT THE PREVIOUS SEASON, MADE ST. CATHARINES TEEPEES JUNIOR A TEAM IN 1961 AS A 19–YEAR–OLD ROOKIE

SIGNED WITH THE CHICAGO BLACK HAWKS ORGANIZATION IN 1962. FIRST CONTRACT PAID $3,800 PLUS A $1,000 SIGNING BONUS

TRADED IN 1967 WITH KEN HODGE AND FRED STANFIELD TO THE BOSTON BRUINS FOR PIT MARTIN, JACK NORRIS AND GILLES MAROTTE

BECAME FIRST PLAYER IN NHL TO REACH "THE CENTURY MARK," WITH 49 GOALS AND 77 ASSISTS FOR 126 POINTS IN THE 1968–69 SEASON

SCORED A THEN–RECORD 76 GOALS AND 76 ASSISTS IN 78 GAMES DURING THE 1970–71 SEASON

HELPED LEAD BRUINS TO STANLEY CUPS IN 1970 AND 1972

ELECTED TO THE NHL FIRST ALL–STAR TEAM EACH YEAR FROM 1969 TO 1974, AND TWICE TO THE SECOND ALL–STAR TEAM, IN 1968 AND 1975

WON THE ART ROSS TROPHY, THE REGULAR–SEASON POINT–SCORING TITLE, FIVE TIMES, IN 1969 AND FROM 1971–74

WON THE HART TROPHY, THE LEAGUE'S MOST VALUABLE PLAYER AWARD, IN 1969 AND 1974

WON THE LESTER B. PEARSON AWARD, THE LEAGUE'S OUTSTANDING PLAYER AS SELECTED BY THE NHL PLAYERS' ASSOCIATION, IN 1971 AND 1974

WON THE LESTER PATRICK TROPHY, FOR OUTSTANDING SERVICE TO HOCKEY IN THE UNITED STATES, IN 1978

SKATED IN 10 NHL ALL–STAR GAMES

NOTCHED 717 GOALS AND 873 ASSISTS FOR 1,590 POINTS IN 1,282 REGULAR–SEASON GAMES

TRADED FROM BOSTON TO THE NEW YORK RANGERS IN 1975 WITH CAROL VADNAIS FOR BRAD PARK, JEAN RATELLE AND JOE ZANUSSI

ACQUIRED NICKNAME "TRADER PHIL" AS WHEELER–DEALER GM FOR THREE SEASONS IN THE LATE 1980S WITH THE NEW YORK RANGERS

FIRST GM OF THE EXPANSION TAMPA BAY LIGHTNING

INDUCTED INTO THE HOCKEY HALL OF FAME IN 1984

Acknowledgements

I would like to express special gratitude to Michelle Benjamin of Raincoast for her faith in the Remembering series, and to editor Derek Fairbridge for his smart, judicious story editing. Thanks also to my contributors, Frank Orr, Rob Adler and Doug Herod, and to the *St. Catharines Standard* — the newspaper where I began my career as a reporter in the late 1970s — for allowing us to use their archival photos of Phil Esposito as a junior with the 1961–62 St. Catharines Teepees, an all but forgotten team that included such future NHL stars as Dennis Hull, Ken Hodge and Roger Crozier.

Thanks also to my longtime collaborator and art director Bill Douglas, whose bright, stylish layouts have enlivened the pages of all five titles in this series. And a big tip of the hockey helmet to former Stoddart editor Jim Gifford, who loves this series as much as I do and whose advice helped keep it on the rails when it seemed we'd jumped the track.

Thanks also to my best hockey pal Dylan McMahon, and to my wife, Liza, who happily drives the 120 km from Toronto to Oshawa and back to cheer for "our team," the OHL's Oshawa Generals.

Finally, thanks to Craig Campbell of the Hockey Hall of Fame for furnishing countless pictures of Espo as a Bruin, a Ranger, a Black Hawk and a member of Team Canada.

Grateful acknowledgement is made to the the Hockey Hall of Fame for use of all photographs used on the jacket and inside of this book with the exceptions of pages 4 and 7, courtesy of the *St. Catharines Standard*.

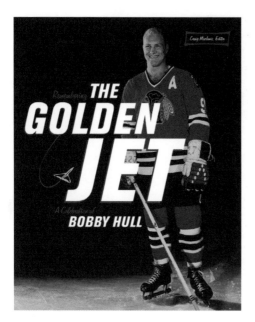

ALSO AVAILABLE

REMEMBERING THE GOLDEN JET

Craig MacInnis, Editor

His blistering slapshot revolutionized the game. He led what some argue was the best team in NHL history — the 1960–61 Chicago Black Hawks — to a Stanley Cup victory. He was the ultimate combination of power, speed and intimidation. Two decades after his retirement, Bobby Hull remains one of the most colourful characters in hockey, a high-flying icon in a game with few new superheroes. Here is a rare and compelling tribute to the man who transcended the game and touched hockey fans everywhere.

1-55192-633-4 $24.95 CDN • $16.95 US

RAINCOAST BOOKS
www.raincoast.com

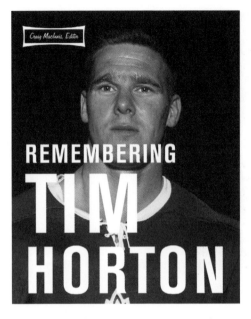

ALSO AVAILABLE

REMEMBERING TIM HORTON

Craig MacInnis, Editor

For 18 years, Tim Horton captained a stellar Toronto Maple Leaf defensive corps that featured fellow greats Allan Stanley, Bobby Baun and Carl Brewer. Horton, a constant threat to Bobby Hull and other offensive powerhouses of his day, led the Maple Leafs to four Stanley Cups in the 1960s, including the franchise's last Cup win in 1967. The powerful rear guard shared All-Star honours with Bobby Orr and Pierre Pilote, establishing him as one of the best defencemen ever.

1-55192-631-8 $24.95 CDN • $16.95 US

RAINCOAST BOOKS
www.raincoast.com

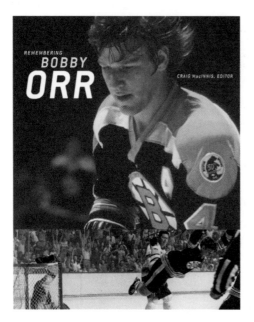

ALSO AVAILABLE

REMEMBERING BOBBY ORR

Craig MacInnis, Editor

Bobby Orr, the best defenceman the hockey world has ever seen, was the unanimous choice for rookie of the year in 1967. Twice he led the NHL in scoring, an unprecedented feat for a player at his position, with an unbelievable 120 and 135 points. He was voted the NHL's most valuable player three years in a row. Orr forever changed the game of hockey, and the lives of those who watched him play.

1-55192-627-x $24.95 CDN • $16.95 US

RAINCOAST BOOKS
www.raincoast.com

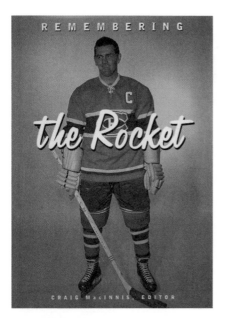

ALSO AVAILABLE

REMEMBERING THE ROCKET

Craig MacInnis, Editor

He has been called the "greatest goal scorer in professional hockey history," not least for his astonishing feat of notching 50 goals in 50 games. Yet that alone hardly explains his legend. Maurice Richard not only ushered in hockey's modern era with his prolific scoring touch and fiery play, he also came to symbolize the hopes and fears of an entire culture. Quebec in the 1940s and 1950s wanted a hero and they found one in Richard — a fierce competitor, a skilled athlete and a proud warrior.

1-55192-629-6 $24.95 CDN • $16.95 US

RAINCOAST BOOKS
www.raincoast.com